SIXTY NOT OUT

Surviving Jay Peak
They Stole His Savings, Not His Spirit

DAVID WOODING

SHINE
PRESS

Tampa, Florida

SHINE
PRESS

Publisher: Shine Press
4522 W. Village Dr. #1294
Tampa, Florida 34624
Shine-Press.com | Jodi@Shine-Press.com
Shine Press is an imprint of Jodi K Costa, LLC.

Disclaimer: This book is a personal account of the author's experiences and perspective. The events, conversations, and situations described are based on his life, and while he has made every effort to present them as accurately as possible, they are filtered through his personal lens.

For speaking engagements, event invitations, bulk orders, and other author requests, please contact the publisher: Jodi@Shine-Press.com

F I R S T   E D I T I O N

ISBN: 979-8-9937924-6-0

Shine Press offers writing, editing, designing, publishing, and marketing services, focusing on high quality at affordable prices with an excellent author experience.

Contact us for more information about our personalized Spark Books, publishing packages, book marketing, and Bestseller Campaign.

I dedicate this book to the four most important people in my life.
Vanessa, Georgiana, Olivia, and Tahlia.

And in memory of my parents.
Olive Wooding and Peter Wooding.

Contents

1

Wake Up Call

Okay, when your wife of nearly 30 years calls you into the room, looks you square between the eyes and says that if you don't sort your shit out, she's leaving, you sort of take notice.

I kid you not, this happened to me maybe five weeks ago. It's a bit of a double whammy really. I'd just celebrated my 60th birthday; it wasn't a biggie for me, but I never saw this conversation coming. Initially I brushed it off and thought she was just saying it to get some sort of reaction. I'd always thought we were the perfect, strong, solid, locked-in couple. I still believe that. This was her way to fire a warning shot over the bow, so to speak. It was a threat, but it was done from kindness. I know it was done from kindness, from love, and obviously for the betterment of our family.

I've always been a happy, jolly sort of chap, able to brush small things off. I was also able to brush big things off. Over the past few years...around the time my father died...I began to change. Turning sixty didn't seem to bother me on the surface, but perhaps it affected me more than I realized, as I drifted into periods of depression without fully understanding the toll it would take. The people I cherish most...my family and the few close friends I have...were the ones quietly

"

feeling the impact. It's a gentle, gradual process which needs someone on the outside to call it. I don't think I saw it myself until that time.

It was probably a combination of three things. Bad luck, definitely bad luck as you will see later. Age, in the respect that I think your brain diagnoses and deals with issues differently when you get older. Thirdly, the "mild" depression which I was in and which had just been highlighted to me. I don't think you can do anything about two of those. I obviously can't stop my biological clock ticking, that's inevitable. As for the bad luck, I don't really think, in retrospect, I could have done anything about that. You make your choices at the time based on all available information, rightly or wrongly, it's only later, when you are fully committed to something that someone decides to take a big dump on you. Anyway, you'll be the judge of that.

I guess the only thing I can do something about is the depression side, which I have to address first. I have to work through it and make a conscious effort to pull myself out of the hole I've found myself in. It's not going to be easy, I don't imagine, for one minute. Especially coming from a family that traditionally bottled things up, kept things inside, a family that didn't share their feelings. It's going to have to be a huge shift change for me to open up, be honest, be vocal, share, to deal with this head on, because unless I deal with it head on, I feel like it will fully consume me, and we don't want to go there. We don't want that to happen.

The first step is acknowledging, which I've done. The book I'm writing and hopefully finishing, will be cathartic. I'm pretty sure that's the right word. I'll check it out, but if it is the right word, I'm using it. I'll stick to "cathartic." It's going to be a catalyst for me to do better, to try harder, to really embrace life, because hey, let's face it, I'm 60, but I've got a lot more living to do with my wife.

I know the external perception of me and my family is very different to the reality that we are going through. On the surface we look like we are successful, comfortable, and dare I say, well off. Below the surface it's a different story, very similar to the duck that's sailing through life, carefree, all serene on the surface,

SIXTY NOT OUT

while below the waterline, out of sight of everyone, his little feet are frantically struggling to keep him afloat, struggling to help him survive. It's time for me to break the perception and expose the real me that has been in denial for so long. Time to acknowledge the damage that thirteen years of renting has done, not only to our financial stability, but also how it stripped us of any sense of belonging, any sense of community, and most devastating of all, any sense of security that a parent wants so badly to provide for his wife and children. It's hard to quell the feeling I have somehow failed them in one of life's most fundamental needs.

I know I had bottled things up for nearly ten years, and the cracks were starting to show. I've heard of people writing down all their frustrations and anger on paper and then burning them on a mountaintop or something similar. We don't really have mountains in Florida, so this book is going to be my sounding board, my turning point. Maybe by trying to balance all my fury and sadness with the overwhelming amount of happiness I had in my earlier years, I will see things from a new perspective. I am determined not to be defined by the last ten years. I owe that to myself, my family, and to my future.

Oh, did I forget to mention that $500,000 was embezzled from us and we had to move on from over 15 rental properties? Throughout the whole process, never evicted I might add, we still found time to raise our three wonderful daughters and remain married amid all the chaos.

Like any good book does, and to help understand how we got to this point, we have to go back to the beginning, where it all started. Let the therapy begin.

2

The Early Years

Someone once said that if you don't remember your childhood, then you probably had a good one. I believe the basis is that you only remember traumatic events when you're younger. They tend to stick in your mind and I guess shape your early years. Based on that, in my early years I would summarise I probably had a good childhood. There were no real major traumas or upsets, at least not until my later teen years. Anything up until the age of 15 or 16 was pretty much run of the mill.

The only traumatic event I do remember didn't actually happen to me, it happened to our cat. It was traumatic for her. We had some wheat fields at the back of our house and my brother and I used to enjoy running through them in the autumn just before they were harvested. Our cat followed suit and also enjoyed running through them. One day we noticed the combine harvester entering the field and decided it was time to make a quick exit. The cat didn't make the same sensible decision. Suffice to say we saw the cat in the morning but, unfortunately, we did not see the cat again in the evening, or in fact ever. The Wooding family consensus was that the cat and the combine harvester had a coming together and there was only ever going to be one winner, unfortunately it wasn't the cat. In memory of her I always use her as the answer to one of those *reset password* questions you have. What was the name of your first pet? Smokey is now immortal and living her best life in a hay bale in the sky.

I was born into a typical middle class family in the Midlands in the UK, Wolverhampton to be exact, although I do remember telling most people I was from Staffordshire because Wolverhampton had the reputation for being a little bit more down market than Stafford or Staffordshire. I guess even at an early age I was aware of people's perceptions and where you said you came from mattered. I wouldn't say I was ashamed of where I was from, but I definitely didn't promote where I was from, let's put it that way.

I actually lived in a little village, which was eight miles from Wolverhampton and ten or eleven from the county town of Stafford. I overlooked the mileage difference and tended to veer more onto the Stafford side of things, so when people asked me where I was from, it was easier to say Stafford or Staffordshire than Wolverhampton. I guess early snobbery coming out there, which I didn't know existed until I'm thinking about it now, because no one ever told me to say that. It was just something I intuitively knew what to do, or thought I knew what to do, to present myself in the best possible light.

My dad worked at the local newspaper as a sub editor for many, many years. I actually thought it was a very important job he held. Knowing that the editor of the newspaper was the top guy, if you were the sub editor, in my mind at the time, I thought he was probably second in control, or second in command, or second in whatever he did at work. It was only a little bit further down the line I realised there were quite a few sub editors employed by the newspaper. What his job involved was collating all the stories onto a page. He was allocated certain pages which were his responsibility. Stories came in and he arranged them on the page and sent them down to the printing department to get them printed. He did that, five days a week. He worked very hard, never moaning about work, and was happy to do his job.

My mum had a part-time job. I'm assuming she was trained but I really must admit that I don't know that for a fact. Anyway, she had a special skill with

                    SIXTY NOT OUT

numbers, numeracy and accounting, so she worked two or three days a week, also in Wolverhampton, at an accounting firm. I think that was also done just because, being a typical middle class family, we needed two wages coming in. We had the two cars, a nice detached home overlooking some fields and a football pitch where the local village team used to play, if I remember.

We took your typical holidays, all quintessentially English, two weeks half board in either Cornwall or Devon, all very popular with middle class Midlanders. We would drive down the M5 in a beat up old Maxi. I seem to remember the colour being sun faded red. We also had a nondescript coloured Morris 1100 which made the journey on a couple of occasions. That car used to make the most un-car-like sounds. I'm surprised we made it all in one piece. I do remember on one occasion being sworn to secrecy by my dad that, in the unlikely event we were pulled over for speeding, not to tell the officer that the speedo wasn't working and hadn't been for over three months. After all, how was he to know we were going over the limit when the dial was showing 0mph? I was happy to keep that secret. Bending the law a little for one's own benefit can't be all wrong, can it?

Mum's cars were a different story. I can only remember two. A classic Ford Anglia and, very out of keeping with the frugal Wooding mentality, an extremely impressive racing green Sunbeam Alpine, registration 908 FJW. A private plate before private plates were a thing. The car was just super old and registered before they even thought about putting yearly letters at the front or end of the reg. Knowing what I know now, how cool would it have been to keep the car and name my first born Freddy Jack Wooding? Great christening present that would have made.

It's strange looking back, but I can't actually remember my mum ever driving. I guess she must have to get to work, but that memory is just not there. She also used to dream about retiring and touring around Europe in a classic Mercedes 350SL. Now that's a dream I can relate to.

I remember we did go to Spain once, but on a plane. Mercedes would have been too small. It was one of the first package holidays and I was probably about nine years old. We couldn't afford to go during the school holidays, so I remember we went out of school in October because it was obviously a lot cheaper. That was also my first time on an aeroplane. Costa Brava, that's where we went. We flew into Girona, pronounced Hirona, and it was my first time in a proper hotel as well. The first time being served by Spanish waiters and waitresses, it was great, all very new and exciting.

Then a few years later we followed up that European excursion with a camping trip to Greece, which was also fun. It was extremely hot, I remember, as we could afford to go in the height of summer because camping holidays were quite a lot cheaper than holidays with hotels. The heat was so intense we all slept outside looking up at the stars and also at the planes landing at the nearby airport until about midnight. I seem to remember my dad mentioning it on many occasions.

I never appreciated how cool that was at the time and I don't think I've ever done it since, which seems crazy. Maybe the heat, noise and mosquitoes took a lasting toll after all.

School was normal, whether that's a good thing or not remains to be seen. In retrospect I wish I had embraced it more and pushed a few boundaries, but it wasn't in my genetic make-up at the time, so I was content that my childhood school was normal. Nothing major to report.

Apart from a mental perspective, that is. I think that was possibly the first time I became a little bit self-conscious of my body, which has stayed with me for a large portion of my years, but it was something that in my early days, and definitely while I was at school, caused me quite a bit of anxiety.

For as long as I can remember, I've always had a lot of freckles and quite a few moles on my body. The moles were, or are, hereditary, although my parents didn't seem to have a lot of moles. One thing I do know for certain is that my sunbathing habits were a huge factor with my freckles. I tended to burn any opportunity I had. That makes it sound like I didn't have a choice, but I did, I just chose to ignore it. I would lie in my back garden with the sole reason of getting a suntan. I wasn't patient, so I tended to overcook myself. Stupid, crazy, ignoring all the advice to avoid midday sun and always wear a high factor lotion. It all fell on deaf ears. All that mattered was image and trying to look cool. Who gave a damn that in 30 years time your skin would look like shit? Didn't matter in the crazy days of the 80s. Anyway, 30 years was a lifetime away and I wanted to look good tonight, at the expense of my older self. That was a small price to pay. Live for the moment, right?

Back in the day people thought that the browner your skin tone was, or the more tan you were, that it was a healthy look. Obviously we all know now that this is the complete opposite of what healthy is. I remember sunbathing with no sign of any suncream or sun factor anywhere. Baby oil and lemon juice were standard practice for tanning, I even remember some of the lemon juice used to go in my hair because I thought it would give me that blonde surf look. Needless to say it never worked. My hair always stayed super dark, but it used to smell all shades of funky. But you know, things you do when you are young.

Anyway, the upshot was I used to get burnt quite a lot on my shoulders and on my chest. I would blister up and I could never leave the peeling skin alone, so I would always pick at it and pull it, which would expose sort of undeveloped skin below which was still very red. Freckles would start to appear from nowhere, not small freckles either, big, irregular shaped ones like four-leaved clovers. They were brown, however, not green like regular four-leaved clovers. Now that would have been weird.

It's only in later life that my natural aging process caught up with my body and they've actually sort of all blended in now and I'm not conscious of them anymore. All the moles have been sliced and diced by my dermatologist. Who would have thought I'd still be paying for my vanity all these years later, both in health and monetary terms?

Financially speaking, my dermatologist is pleased that myself and a lot of other narrow minded 80s kids were short sighted enough to fry in the midday sun. Another saying springs to mind. Only mad dogs and Englishmen go out in the midday sun. I'm one of those. Woof, woof.

It always seemed easier to hide behind a suntan, but again that goes back to a confidence thing which you naturally get as you start to get into later life, a sort of don't give a shit attitude. But I know at the time I was acutely conscious of my freckles and would cover up and hide them at every opportunity I had.

I used to play on the soccer team with my high school. I would always get changed at the last minute or rush to put my shirt on and off when most other people were either not looking. I was always scoping the room out to see the most advantageous opportunity to not expose myself to my fellow teammates because, as we all know, kids can be very, very cruel. I guess I would try to protect myself from that. I would hear people making the odd comment about how I had a lot of freckles. Let's play join the dots. I was called *moly* maybe a couple of times, which all adds to the self-consciousness we have about our body. So any opportunity I had I would probably cover up. I would never be confident about swimming because of having to obviously wear either shorts or swimming trunks, which were very popular at the time, believe it or not.

If you combine that with a distinct inability to carry any muscle or tone up in any way, my body image in my own mind was a skinny, scrawny, lanky kid with freckles and moles, who was much more comfortable being covered up and keeping to the shadows at any opportunity.

It wasn't all pessimistic, however. I was always aware, and made aware by other people, that I had a relatively attractive, handsome face. From the neck down I was embarrassed, but from the neck up I was quite proud and confident of the face that I was born with.

School passed by rather monotonously. I was an average B grade student, had a bunch of B grade friends and played on the second string football team, which I suppose was also B level. I just put my head down, did my work, didn't overwork, didn't really bring anything extra to the table, just did what I had to do to get by.

I made sure I passed my exams and was acutely aware at the time that the social side of school was something I enjoyed. So between lessons or on school lunches, being able to walk around the school, especially as you became more of a senior in the school, smiling at groups of girls and hanging out with my friends, being lads if you will, was always something which was fun. I really enjoyed that boy-girl interaction on a very surface level, admiring from a distance and, I suppose, being admired from a distance.

I don't think I got into too much trouble. Never had a detention, didn't skip school at all, never skipped, always went when I had to go. The only real incident that I can remember was myself and a friend being picked on by a couple of the school bullies. Every school has a group of ten or twelve lads that carry themselves differently. They take pleasure in intimidating people and basically work their way through everyone else in the school to assert their power, if that's what they think power is, by picking on, intimidating and ultimately punching anyone else that was deemed a threat or they felt needed taking down a notch or two.

I don't think threat is probably the right word, more of an inconvenience that someone else was getting more airtime than them. You raise your head up above the pulpit and they were there to knock it off, quite literally. I was never a threat to anyone because I wasn't a physical guy. As I said before, with my frame I wasn't physical, but I was probably getting onto the radar a little more than was comfortable for them, being a popular lad with the girls. I suppose any sort of popularity aimed at boys that wasn't them sort of becomes a threat which had to be dealt with.

The rumour started to spread that these guys were going to get us at one of the breaks, me and my friend. We laid low initially and managed to avoid them for a day or so because we knew what was coming, but eventually we realised it was a fruitless task because the word was out that it was our time to be picked on.

I remember putting ourselves in the crosshairs. We just went to sit on a little wall and we knew that these two guys, the so-called tough guys at the school, would know where we were. Then they just came up to us with a little smile on their faces, said "hi boys" and started swinging.

I don't actually think my assailant managed to land a punch. My friend got off a little worse than me. The guy swung at me and I sort of ducked down out of the way and managed to grab him around the waist or something. Then I think we fell over. One thing I actually remember is someone laughing afterwards because they said I actually tried to kick the guy, which wasn't my intention. I was very submissive and my mindset was I just would have taken whatever it was just to get it out the way. But when it actually came to it, when I actually was threatened, then my fight or flight started kicking in, literally. I didn't make a very good account of myself, but I did manage to suppress the other guy, so I came out with a little bit of credibility, hopefully.

It was broken up pretty quickly by some teachers, we all got hauled in front of the headmaster, who obviously was aware that these two guys did this on a regular basis. They had obviously been in front of him many times and he realised that my friend and I were just the latest two victims. I think he had a couple of witnesses to speak to as well, who coincidentally were friends of the two aggressors. Two little scrawny kids, I seem to remember, standing outside the door making comments when we walked in, obviously empowered by the fact that they were protected by the two bullies. They would never say that if it was just a one on one situation, which makes me smile now because I can see through that completely.

But it blew over pretty quickly. We were flavour of the month for a week or so, they had their wrists slapped and we all moved on. They moved on to picking on someone else. I tried to avoid them the rest of the school year, which was quite easy because they played truant a lot and didn't go to school most of the time.

I don't know what they are doing now and I don't really care. It was their way of getting through school. Whatever works, right?

     SIXTY NOT OUT

Needless to say, I don't think it had any effect on my growing popularity, which probably pissed them off, but that's the way the cookie crumbles, I guess.

The only other run-in I had with bullies, or guys that thought they could pick on other people, was a very strange tradition we had in our school, which is possible it happens in all of the schools in the UK, or at least did. On the last day of school the guys in the fifth year, which I guess we would call seniors, would basically have license, not by the teachers obviously but their own license, to go around school and basically thump, kick or punch anyone they particularly didn't like over their five years of school. The majority of them obviously being younger because they were the oldest in the school.

They would have this license, a warped sense of entitlement that they believed they could just walk around the corridors between lessons and during lunch break, hunt people down, target people. It was just like a free hall pass, whack-a-mole on steroids. Basically they could do whatever they wanted, there would be no consequences, no repercussions, because they had finished school anyway. They had taken their exams, if they actually were clever enough to take exams that is.

I remember there was this one guy from the little village next to me. Again, the word on the street was that I was in his crosshairs. I don't know why. I didn't really know him and I didn't think he knew me, but I just made sure I stayed out of his way for the last day of school. He left school with one less punch on his ticket and I avoided another unfair beating.

I can wholeheartedly say that when my time came to leave school it was done without any punches. After all, I was college bound and it wasn't the done thing to punch people at college.

As much as school was about structure, conforming and fitting in, I feel college gave me the ability to do the complete opposite. Freedom, fun, and unregulated relaxation. With my new drivers licence, I gained the ability to come and go on my own - such a priviledge after the constraints of school.

A lot of that was down to my very first car, nothing special, nothing expensive, in true Wooding style. It was a little Mini, strange colour, sort of off greeny yellow, slightly dirty effect. That didn't last too long. We had bought it, well my dad had bought it from someone in Wolverhampton but it was actually an Irish import with an Irish number plate.

There was a lot of trouble with the IRA in and around Birmingham at the time, so my dad didn't want to keep an Irish number plate on the car for obvious reasons, probably a sensible idea. We also decided to do away with the horrible mucky mustardy colour that it was, we went for the rather adventurous matte black look. I don't think the paint job was that professional and we ended up with more of a front door gloss kind of finish, complete with brush strokes, but it was better than the green so no complaints here. First car. Cost no more than 500 pounds. Pretty cool to have my own wheels.

At the time, in the early 80s, it was all on trend to have the furry dice hanging from the mirror, honestly, which I did, and I even had the exceptionally long fluorescent green aerial which was attached to the back bumper. It was probably about 12 feet long, it bent forward and clipped to a little clip on the roof rail just above the driving door. That was the done thing, again honestly.

I also had a Radio 1 sun visor which stretched the whole length of the windscreen, back in the 275, 285 days, so I actually feel like I was pretty cool. I challenge anyone out there to tell me that, at the time, it wasn't a good look. Super awesome to be driving down the street with your window down, manual radio sort of tuned into a crackly station, then you flick the aerial off its clip, watch it spring back, and that was freedom right there in a nutshell. That was my ride back and forth to college five days a week and to the pub at least four times a week for the next two years.

I charted a safe passage through college, more by design than luck. I didn't really want to stretch myself too much. I chose a business diploma course because it covered many different business concepts and, as I didn't know what I wanted to do with my life, other than being a businessman of some sort, I remember

                    SIXTY NOT OUT

enjoying the marketing side of it. We obviously did a little bit of economics, psychology and accounting. Wow, accounting, that was tedious. Sorry Mum. I definitely enjoyed the promotion, advertising and marketing side of the business course as that was something that really interested me and I felt probably, for the first time in my life, that was an area I wanted to pursue.

The college work was easy. I didn't have to strain myself, so my plan worked. We had rolling assessments, so no real emphasis on a final exam, so in typical Dave style I passed that diploma. I think I got probably a B, surprisingly, which was par for the course, or slightly better than par if we are splitting hairs.

Looking back, my college years were more about the social side, having fun, going out, meeting people. I enjoyed the common room elements at the college. We had a table football game there, which was great, a cheap cafeteria and lots of us students just having fun.

College also introduced me to a huge cross section of people. It was all inclusive. You would have the sensible, studious, nerdy types that treated it as an extension of school, but you would also have an eclectic mix, older arty types and sportspeople who didn't give a shit about learning, who would add something extra to our lectures.

I remember one guy in particular, Tim. He was a rugby player and about five years older than me. He was from a successful family so had no real ambition to learn. He would just rock back on his chair in the middle of a lesson and start singing. Really remarkably random. He would always sing the same song which I, of course, remember off by heart.

I used to sing it to the girls when they were too young to understand. I then took a hiatus when they would have understood, very inappropriate, and in later life I've found myself singing it again in times of frivolity, always with a smile on my face.

I guess you are dying to know what it is now. A small pre-warning, it's not quite as bad as the one I used to sing to the girls about the three pussies. Hey pussy, ho pussy. It's a genuine kids book I swear and I stopped singing it when they started to talk, in front of them anyway. I still sing it in front of Vanessa. I think she kind of likes it. I'm weird, right? Anyway, back to Tim's song.

"My girl's got ginger hair underneath her underwear, I know coz I've been there. She's my baby now."

I'll leave that right there and go back to college life.

I could drive myself in the morning, leave whenever I wanted, obviously after my classes. I didn't have too much homework, if any at all, and I enjoyed the nightlife that Stafford offered at the time. There were a couple of really popular little pubs in town. I'll try to remember what it was called that we always used to go to on the island. Christmas week was the highlight of the year. They used to have discos every afternoon, that's funny, discos, on Monday, Tuesday, Wednesday, Thursday. Malt and Hops, it just came to me. That was the name of the pub on the island.

The discos were at the Riverside recreational facility, very basic, a DJ and cheap booze, the perfect combination for a fun filled afternoon. Then on the last day of Christmas week and when we graduated, everyone always used to go to the Malt and Hops early doors, sampling fine ales, pork scratchings and Scotch eggs. Highly intoxicated, we would walk round the corner to the ultimate in nightclub glitz and glam, Top of the World, to drink ourselves into even more of a stupor.

Crazy as it may seem, I would then venture back to my trusty little black Mini and drive the eight miles home. I know I shouldn't have driven home. Crazy choice, but this is way before anyone had even thought of ride sharing. Taxis were super expensive and the bus just wasn't an option. Definitely not cool catching the bus.

Not clever and not smart, but at the time and under the influence you make reckless choices and you don't feel that you can do anything wrong.

        SIXTY NOT OUT

Needless to say I didn't do it again. That would be ridiculous. By year two I had to change my ways, which I did.

That year I drove home in my new Triumph Spitfire 1500, and when I say new I mean new to me, not new new. It was probably about ten years old, just old enough for things to start going wrong, and by things going wrong I mean big things. It was a crazy orange colour. What is that with me in the early years of driving and weird car colours?

I guess all the ugly coloured cars were cheaper. Beggars can't be choosers, right?

I hadn't just switched out my car in the second year of college, I also changed girlfriends. Wow, first mention of girlfriends. Buckle up, here we go.

My first real relationship was exactly as you would imagine it. A bit clumsy at times, if you know what I mean, a bit awkward most of the time, especially considering I still had doubts about my body image, so didn't have the confidence to build the physical side of the relationship, which, as I now know, is a very important factor in creating a strong bond. I feel that was missing in girlfriend number one.

I'm not being flippant or disrespectful calling her number one, as I'm aware she has feelings, but I just want to protect her privacy. I got on well with her family. I learned early on that the basis of establishing a good relationship was getting the family on side. A strange backhanded way of building a relationship with a girl I suppose. I would have been better served concentrating more on the girl and less on the family. Anyway, it seemed to work for me, so with anyone I had strong feelings for and could see a future with, I always went to the trusted family playbook.

We lasted somewhere between two and three years, but as my memory is not what it used to be, I'm going to box it up, say we just ran our course and moved on. The five things that always spring to mind when I think of her are:

The Lexicon of Love by ABC.

Plumbing.

Inverted nipple.

Cannock.

Older sister.

In no particular order, and I'm just going to leave that there.

Along with the second year of college and the second car came the second girlfriend, and if I'm to say she was the polar opposite of my first girlfriend then I would not be lying.

She was a little younger than me, maybe four years. This was a trend that continued for the rest of time, as you will see. She was a local Stafford girl and I'm going to be honest, I cannot remember how we met. She was an aspiring model and well known in the town. We got pretty close pretty quick and had a lot of fun just enjoying life. We settled into the relationship thing quite easily. I got on well with her family, which obviously meant we were on course for a long term relationship. Stay tuned.

College came and went and all of a sudden, there I was with the big wide world of adulthood ahead of me with no clue what I wanted to do, apart from the rough idea that I wanted to work for myself. Early 80s, the time of YOPs and enterprise allowance, or unemployment. I chose the enterprise allowance, partly because of the 80 pounds I would receive every two weeks, but mainly for the fact that it would let me set up my own business. The birth of the entrepreneur happened right there.

Maybe that should read wannabe entrepreneur.

The Window Cleaner

I cannot remember the complete criteria of the Enterprise Allowance Scheme other than you got 80 pounds every two weeks and you either got a 2,000 pound grant or you had to invest 2,000 pounds. Either way, I ended up with a set of ladders, two buckets, some sponges, chammy leathers and a tube of Fairy liquid. Oh, and a new red Ford Escort, and by new I mean new to me.

I was well into negative equity with the Spitfire. The culmination of numerous trips over to Stafford to see my girlfriend, my driving habits and the fact that it was far beyond its prime all combined for the perfect storm, which was to blow my once pride and joy all the way to the scrap heap. I should have seen the writing on the wall when I had to change the carburettor and replace the whole rear axle after the back left wheel just collapsed going round a corner, all in one week. Is it just me, or did those Spitfire rear wheels sit at a funny angle?

Pair that with the attack of the Krooklok during one of my now more frequent arguments with my girlfriend. This was more mental scarring for the car than physical. Imagine a device invented to protect the car from being stolen doing a complete 180, the audacity, and now being used as a weapon against the car's occupant, otherwise known as me.

To be fair, no contact was made between said Krooklok and either my being
or the car. I think it was wielded more as a threat, as I drove off to avoid any
further confrontation, have I mentioned I don't do confrontation, the Krooklok
ended up bouncing onto the front seat as I sped away, movie style, leaving my
irate and angry girlfriend effing and jeffing in the middle of the road, but more
importantly in my rear view mirror.

This was one of the first arguments we had, but it wasn't the last.

Poor Spitfire. I bet it was glad to get to its final resting place.

Now let me tell you a little bit about window cleaning in a small village. It is a
dangerous pastime.

There was little old me, well actually, lanky, skinny young me, just wanting to
supplement my 40 pounds a week so I could get enough cash to put some petrol
in the car and have a few beers at the weekend. It wasn't enough that I had to
watch whose turf I was moving into in the high rolling window cleaning world,
window cleaning mafia was alive and real, I also had to look out for something far
more dangerous, the bored housewife.

OK, let me paint the scene, non confrontational Dave, the local boy, up a
ladder when a couple of, let's say, undesirable male specimens from the next
not as affluent village start shaking the ladder from below and, leaving out
the expletives, tell you in an aggressive direct manner that if I start poaching
their clients then there would be trouble. I'm sure I muttered something in an
apologetic tone and assured them that was not my intention. After all, faced with
the choice of having me clean their windows or these two meat heads, I'm sure
the homeowner was left with no doubt who to choose.

I didn't tell them that, why would I? But I'm sure I thought about it, either
at the time or later that night, as is usually the case. How many times have we
all thought, I wish I had said this in a certain situation, that would have been so
funny. It's just, at the time, usually through fear, our brains freeze up and we are
lucky if we get a whimper out.

     SIXTY NOT OUT

Anyway, I had learned my lesson and vowed not to poach any of the meat heads' customers. They were all pretty shitty homes anyway, filled with more meat heads. I set my sights higher, bigger houses, more windows, which meant more money. The only downside to that, which I was to find out, was that bigger houses meant the housewives were even more bored, and there was the potential for trouble.

Ambition has always been one of my qualities, but like anything in life it ebbs and flows at different times. It has seasons, shall we say.

During my window cleaning years my ambition was definitely subdued. I was still unsure of what direction my life was going to take, so I was in a treading water phase, happy to "get by".

I was sure I didn't want to be a window cleaner all my life. It crossed my mind to build up and develop a huge round with the potential to sell it for thousands of pounds, but that spark was never really there, so I stayed in my lane and "got by".

The Enterprise Allowance expired after two years and by that time the business was supposed to be able to stand on its own. I knew that was never going to happen for me. Combine the lack of opportunity with the lack of effort and this baby was always going to blow itself out. The winters were too long, too cold and too wet to ever believe I could create anything worth selling. The writing was on the wall.

The summers were fun but too short. I remember going out to work in the early morning, two buckets in hand, spring in my step. On the rare occasion a pair of denim shorts would be worn, but that just reinforced the age old superstition of never walking under ladders. It would have been a sight for sore eyes.

By now I had established a nice round, comfortable, shall we say. I had a good relationship with most of my customers. Many would make me a drink, most knew my name. They would leave my money in a little envelope for me with my name on.

On the odd occasion I would be asked to clean the inside windows as well, which I was happy to oblige with. I know you can see where I am going with this and you are expecting some great sexual tryst to land just about now. I am sorry to disappoint you. I'm also a little disappointed that it didn't happen also, especially now looking back. It's not that I didn't have the opportunity, well not really an opportunity, more of a situation that if I had handled it differently then maybe it would have led to an opportunity. All very vague and lots of ifs and maybes.

I just didn't have the game at the time to realise that there may have been an opportunity. Don't forget I was still a little awkward about my physicality. Also, I was aware everyone knew me in the small village we lived in and that gossip spread like wildfire. The fact that they were both married also played a big factor.

Let's get things straight. This wasn't an opportunity for me with two married ladies at the same time. These were two individual situations which just didn't materialise.

The first was more of a feeling, you know when you have a strange buzz when you are in someone else's presence. She was an attractive lady whose husband ran a successful business in the village. He travelled a lot and I just happened to clean her windows when he was out of town. It was all a bit flirtatious and I just don't think I had the experience or knowledge to read between the lines. It was a fleeting moment and one that I didn't act on. I think it was only later, when I analysed the interaction, that I realised I had a green light if I had in fact been in my car, engine running, and put it into gear.

My car may as well have been locked up at home in the garage with a dust cloth over it for all the reading between the lines that I was doing.

Number two opportunity was a little more obvious.

I had a routine. I would do the same houses every day on a two week cycle so they would know when to expect me, give or take 30 minutes either way. Reliable as clockwork, me. One lady, let's call her the 2nd Tuesday morning lady, known to be a little bit of a lush, in an unhappy marriage, coincidentally happened to walk out of her bathroom dressed in just a towel, wet hair, just as I was starting her upstairs bedroom window. I'm convinced she knew I was there because I had already said hello to her downstairs as I had started.

She just glanced out the window over my shoulder and gave a small smile, not to me but to the window over my shoulder. She sat down and began to brush her hair.

Again, I didn't react. Not sure if I was petrified, too shy or just too naive to connect the dots and act on it. Needless to say, nothing happened and I continued to do her windows every two weeks. I'm not sure if she was just playing with me, but if she was, it worked. Every time I would drive over to her house I would hope that the opportunity would present itself again, I convinced myself I would do better next time. I would spend a little longer cleaning each window, hoping she would present me with another chance to maybe act on it this time around. But you guessed it, it never happened.

Every time I saw her, either cleaning her windows or just casually in the village, she would give me that knowing smile. You missed out, buddy. I had created scenarios of Mrs Robinson in my head, but that was to be one movie I would never star in. I feel I was cast in the part, but I never even showed up to the audition.

4

A Model Is Born

Around the same time that my window cleaning career was starting to wane, an unexpected opportunity arose. I don't know if I mentioned it earlier, but my second girlfriend was also a part time model, on the one occasion I accompanied her to her agent in Birmingham, I ended up having an uncomfortable conversation with the agent about me doing some work. In a nutshell, they had a half day job the following week that they needed a guy for. I was that guy.

They rushed me to a photographer, who coincidentally was the husband of the agent, to get two or three professional shots done. I thought two of the shots were acceptable, but I remember disliking the third. It was a topless shot with me putting one hand behind my head, quintessentially 80s. All I could see was about 10,000 freckles, slight exaggeration obviously, but I was pale and, in my eyes, very weedy looking. I think we all sort of brushed over that picture and concentrated more on the other two. The two where I was fully clothed, and by fully clothed read, covered up.

It's funny, but for all the time I've been a model, I've never booked a job for my body, so I guess that initial insecurity was justified. Again, one small chink in the body image armour.

Luckily for me, the other two pictures were strong enough to secure me the half day job the following week, which happened to be with the same photographer. The upshot was I worked for four hours that next week and earned more money than I did cleaning windows all week, and that's including the 40 pounds Enterprise Allowance money. Bit of a no brainer really. The window cleaning was to be phased out and the modelling phased in. Little did I know at the time, but I had just punched my ticket to travel the world, all on the modelling dime. Very smart decision, if I do say so myself.

By no stretch of the imagination did this happen overnight. The market in Birmingham was quite limited and, as I have done many times subsequently, modelling was something I switched onto the back burner if something better presented itself, either by choice or necessity, In this case it was necessity, and by necessity I mean lack of money, that was the driving factor in me applying for a part time job at a local car dealership. Well, it was in fact the car radio shop adjacent to the car dealership. They were looking for someone to help out a few days a week. Perfect job for the boy who knows nothing about car radios.

Anyone born after 1990 will be completely baffled by the fact that your average car at the time came without any option to play music. Top of the line cars had radios built into the dash, but anyone else had to buy a stand alone radio, and cassette combined if you were favored or rich enough. Add the option of speakers and you were looking at a major dick extension for the majority of the lads in Wolverhampton, and the majority of lads were in desperate need of a dick extension.

In time, I learned my trade. I could distinguish between sub woofers, tweeters and bass, could recommend the best place for aerial placement, could talk about the pros and cons of Pioneer v Kenwood. Hell, I could even book them in to have all the work carried out on site with one of the technicians. I could easily have earned the nickname HiFi Dave if, in fact, they were giving out nicknames, which they were not, sadly.

As part of my daily duties, I also had the honour and privilege of making number plates for the dealership. Over time, I built up a friendly relationship with a few of the people over there, so it came as no surprise that I was asked to apply for one of the jobs that was about to become available.

This was a full time position, working for someone else. Something that I had never done before and, surprisingly, would never do again. It had to be thought about seriously, which I did, and that, combined with a family life that was going through a major upheaval, I took the plunge, manned up and, through my eyes at the time, thought that it would give me some sort of stability.

5

The Charles Clark Choice, a Bad Choice and Ibiza

Here we go. Shift modelling onto the back burner and full speed ahead in the car industry. The parts department to be exact, what a god awful place that was. I was so out of my comfort zone, talking all day to mechanics, panel beaters and everyone else who knew at least five times more than I did about cars, their engines and how it all worked. It's terrible to admit but I had no desire to learn anything about anything that didn't interest me, and cars didn't interest me. To make it worse I had to wear a long blue doctor type coat with a British Leyland logo on the pocket. If you were really someone then you had a black, blue and red biro popping out of your top pocket. It goes without saying I wasn't anyone. No pens for me.

With a little, who am I kidding, a lot of help from colleagues who actually enjoyed being there and who actually knew what they were talking about, I stumbled through. Stumbled through enough to be considered for what I considered the only job worth having, a van sales rep. This didn't mean I was a rep trying to sell vans. It meant I had my escape route out of the building. I would be delivering all the parts that had been ordered through the parts department, through all the competent parts men and women, through my replacement and through all the blue, black and red pen holders. The open road called my name, I was not going to say no.

I started off on what I would consider the best route. It was long but I only got to do one run a day. The van would be loaded up with all sorts of things that I had no clue what they did. I was pretty safe with the obvious, like if I loaded a rear bumper or a bonnet then I could figure out where they went on the car, but a grease covered ball joint left me bewildered.

The great thing was that once all the deliveries were done then I could go straight home in the empty van. And guess what, my route just happened to finish close to my home. I did have to meander about 100 miles through glorious countryside, even into Wales briefly, before getting home. But in pre cell phone Britain, once I was home I was out of reach of my bosses, so 4pm finishes were very common, let me tell you.

I settled into a nice, comfortable routine, which caught the attention of the powers that be. Reading between the lines, and with a twist of modesty, I was highlighted as a person that might go quite far in the automotive world. For me, I highlighted myself as a person that might go far away from the automotive world. It was a means to an end. Typical David, very comfortable, no stress and no responsibility. I believe the management were completely unaware of my lack of motivation and they fast tracked me on my way to bigger and better things.

I was pulled off the grand sightseeing tour of Wales route and thrust rather unspectacularly into the world of express parts delivery. Very fast, very responsive, very stressful and very not much fun.

I was on call to all the big movers in the Wolverhampton auto world, panel beaters, service engineers and mechanics to name but a few. They would call up to say they needed this, that and the other as soon as possible, I basically had to

SIXTY NOT OUT

jump in my speedy little van and try to get it to them within the hour. Let me tell you that before GPS and in the days of paper A-Z roadmaps, I found it an extremely challenging job.

I think a lack of enthusiasm also contributed to slow delivery times. Welcome to Stress City, which in my world equates to my job turning pretty shitty. Final nail in the coffin, time to look for another job, or should I say another adventure.

At the time I was good friends with a guy called Phil. To say he was a little of a wide boy was an understatement. Arthur Daley had nothing on him. This guy had way more than nine lives. I kid you not, he is the person that got pulled on the M6 at 2.30am doing a speed in excess of 110mph, under the influence was cited and somehow never got prosecuted. Now I know this raises way more questions than I have answers for, mainly what the heck was wrong with my judgment to even get into the car with him. To this day I still cannot believe I did, but I did, and I got away with it and, ultimately, he got away with it.

I have subsequently heard many, many stories about Phil and his path through life but I will reserve judgment as it's his story to tell, not mine. All I know is, at the time we had a whole load of fun. We were partners in crime, wingmen to each other. At one stage we likened ourselves to the Wham boys or Crockett and Tubbs from Miami Vice. How that one worked I will never know.

Anyway, as you've probably gathered, Phil had a very unconventional outlook to life and work. He appeared to be very successful at his job, which was sales. In fact, he was so good he would often sell things to people that he couldn't fulfill, which meant every now and then he would need to take a short leave of absence.

One such leave of absence coincided with my vastly diminishing enjoyment of my job. We hatched a plan. We would ditch the dull, cloudy skies of Wolverhampton and spend the summer on an up and coming island called Ibiza.

Let's get the context straight right from the get go. I'm talking about Club 18-30 Ibiza in the mid 80s, Club Tropicana and all that, not the drug fuelled party island it was to later become. I'm not judging, as I also revisited in the 90s and really enjoyed that drug fuelled party island to the max, from what I could remember.

80s Ibiza was the Ku Club in Ibiza Town and Bar Simple, Tropicana Bar, Idea and Es Paradis in San Antonio, all very neon.

Back in Wolverhampton, as we prepared our summer escape, we had hoped to go all summer, or at least until the money ran out. Considering I didn't have any savings, I thought the whole summer thing was probably a bit of a stretch.

On the other hand, Phil always seemed to have lots of money. Strange that.

So I was the problem. Technically I still had a job. In fact I definitely still had a job, but I had no money. And this is when I did two things that I'm not really proud of.

One I convinced myself was quite clever, albeit still super highlighted by my inability to deal with confrontation. If there is an easy, weak or chicken way to do something then that was going to be my first option. Standing in front of someone and speaking my truth was 100 per cent not my thing.

I hatched a plan to pre-write my resignation letter and leave it at home with my mum with instructions to mail it ten days after I arrived in Ibiza. You see, the thing is, I had booked a two week vacation from work and, as far as they were concerned, I was returning.

I never had any intention of returning.

The letter basically said that I was having a fun time and that I had the opportunity to stay all summer, which I was going to do. Thanks for the last two years, all the opportunities and guidance, but basically, do one. It was a premeditated resignation.

　　　　SIXTY NOT OUT

Now on the face of it that may seem a little sketch, but if you pair it with part two of the story you can see it was about to backfire spectacularly.

Did I mention that I had no money to go on my summer adventures?

I've always been the sort of person that will take an opportunity if I have a chance, and some may say I have the ability to create an opportunity, this falls into the latter. As part of my mundane, boring, repetitive job, here I am trying to manufacture an environment that might justify my actions, rather poorly I might add. Back to the matter in hand. As part of my job, that I got paid for, I might add, I built up relationships with people in the account area I serviced. At that time it was people in the arse end of Wolverhampton. Some had the ability to sign deliveries off to their accounts, others, less scrupulous people, had to settle in cash before I could leave the goods.

I know you can see where I'm going with this. A week before my scheduled permanent vacation I delivered a subframe. For those of you that don't know what a subframe is, it's a large, complex piece of steel that basically supports the car body and also is where the wheels are attached.

The guy had called me that morning, explained what he wanted and asked me to deliver. I should have seen the red flag then, but to the best of my ability I sourced what I thought was the correct subframe, loaded it onto the van and set off. Now I can honestly say, hand on my heart, that I had no intention of doing anything on the wrong side of legal. It's just how the cards landed. The opportunity came and I went for it.

He paid with the exact cash, about seventy pounds I seem to remember, and he didn't want a receipt. Well, what's a boy, with no money and a trip to Ibiza supposed to do?

Yes, that's exactly what I did. My heart raced for about five minutes as I drove off, which in retrospect wasn't that long if I compared it to the ten minutes of palpitations I had when my wife and I ran off from a restaurant in Sitges without paying the bill, but that's a different story for a different time.

I actually think I felt quite smug that I had pulled it off. I had zero money, so I fixed the zero money problem. I had developed the ability to pigeonhole situations and move on quite quickly, especially if they are illegal, which makes it sound like I do it a lot, but I don't. Apart from the odd penny sweets from the Stars News shop in Brewood, I don't recall ever stealing anything else, probably because I was just about to get found out.

All seemed to be going well. I had managed to add a little to my illegal proceeds, jetted off to Ibiza and quite quickly found a nightly job in San Antonio at one of the popular bars. If memory serves me right the official term for my job was "propper". Whether that's true or not I'm unsure, but that's what I remember it being called. I'm open to being corrected. In other words, we had to prop our bar, which meant we had a bunch of tickets that we gave out to people, giving them either free entry or a free drink at the bar. 90 per cent of the tickets went to girls, surprisingly. Get the girls in the bar and the boys would follow. It seemed to work, as a seasonal worker we got a basic wage, free beer and free entry into all the clubs, slept most of the day on the beach and worked and partied all night. Dream job.

I don't remember too much of those days in detail, but I do have one memory etched in my mind, and it's to do with food. At the end of every night we would go see a guy called Tony who was selling bocadillos out the back of his Hillman Hunter. I kid you not.

Everything seemed to be coming together nicely. We had settled in, regular work, and as per my instruction, my mum had mailed the pre written resignation letter to my boss. Life was indeed good.

Until it wasn't.

These were the days long before cell phones. In order to call home you had to buy a phone card and find a phone box that would allow international calls. I had told my mum I would call her once a week to check in, more for her benefit as my dad and her were going through a break up which was upsetting. So as a caring

SIXTY NOT OUT

older son I wanted to be responsible and loving towards her. On one of those calls I soon realised that I was doing the complete opposite of being responsible and caring, as she told me my boss had been in touch with her, had passed on a message to call him and mentioned something about a subframe. Oh shit. Island life was about to get real.

I don't know for sure, but I can almost guarantee that before I made that call I would have paced up and down for at least an hour, sweated from every available orifice I could possibly sweat from, delayed, delayed and delayed some more. I'll have a cup of tea first, then I'll call. I'll have a poo first, then I'll call. A quick bite to eat, then I'll call. Eventually I ran out of excuses, picked up the phone and made a very difficult call.

Deny, deny, and if that doesn't work, deny some more. Add a little confusion, throw the word mix up around a few times and see if any of it sticks. Guess what, it didn't.

It was left with no alternative. I either show up in his office the following Monday or the police would be informed.

No brainer. We had to go back. I didn't fancy being a fugitive in Costa del Ibiza, certainly not for seventy pounds.

Phil was happy to return also. He had mended a few bridges back in the UK and opportunity knocked for him. I also think he had managed to burn many bridges in Ibiza, so the timing was perfect. He had one last trick up his sleeve, however.

Back then it was the done thing to sell the return leg of flights. There was a noticeboard with various one way flights back to the UK. We happened to find two back to Birmingham. Me, in my new found moral high ground, petrified to do anything wrong, paid my person with my hard earned pesetas. Phil, on the other hand, concocted some hair brained scheme to get the ticket first and meet up with the guy that evening and pay him then. Huge mistake. We all know Phil wasn't going to do that. Phil got a free ticket home.

Our summer of fun in Ibiza was cut short. Instead of four months we lasted four weeks, but it was an action packed four weeks, what I can remember of it anyway.

Back home with a tan, time to deal with the ongoing subframe saga. I make it sound like a soap opera, but I can assure you, at the time, I was having sleepless nights worrying about it.

It was like time almost stood still as I waited for that Monday showdown to happen.

I convinced myself that if I just kept denying it, saying it was a mistake,that would be my best defence. If, even for a fleeting moment, I hinted that I had done it on purpose, then I was convinced my defence would crumble and not only would I be a thief but also a liar. I could handle being a liar as long as it was only me who knew I was a liar.

The walk of shame is probably the understatement of the year. 8.30 Monday morning came around and it was time to face the music.

Obviously the manager's office was the furthest point from the main entrance, very similar to the placing of the milk in the supermarket. I knew everyone knew why I was back. Not only had I resigned in a cowardly manner, I had also allegedly stolen a subframe. Time to face the music.

The manager's small office felt even more intimidating as he had also invited the finance director and my immediate boss to head up the interrogation trifecta. I was given multiple opportunities to admit what I had done, but I stuck to my story that it had been a mistake and a misunderstanding, eventually they realised they were not going to get the confession they wanted. I was unceremoniously told to leave the premises and never return, which was alright with me as I had no intention of returning anyway.

It was one of those life lessons you wish you didn't have to learn the hard way, but those are the ones that stay with you forever. A bit like when I bought a pack

SIXTY NOT OUT

of 20 Embassy No.1s at age 14 and proceeded to smoke them all in a wood, threw up violently for 24 hours and subsequently never smoked again. Well, I never bought a pack again. I did have the occasional puff later in life, if you know what I mean.

Or the time that me and Phil, yes bloody Phil again, stumbled across a bottle of Bell's Whisky at a house party we went to and thought we were super sophisticated at fifteen. We must have drunk almost half a bottle each. He seemed to handle his quite well. Me, however, threw up constantly for about 36 hours, so much so that I didn't go home all weekend. Again, life lessons learned the hard way. Ever since that day, 45 years ago, I have never been able to drink any whisky based drink, for which my liver is eternally grateful.

I have also never inadvertently stolen any more subframes. Quite the opposite in fact. I once returned a vintage Rolex I found down the side of a couch in a coffee shop in Manchester to one of the staff. For a split second it crossed my mind to just slip it in my pocket, but I remember seeing an older gentleman leave from that area just as we walked in. He was definitely a Rolex wearing sort of guy, so I did the right thing. I can't speak to the honesty of the staff member I gave it to, but I feel convinced that the gentleman would return once he found out it was missing. I mean, come on, those things are worth a fortune, let alone the sentimental attachment he would have had to it. I'm still too nervous to research the value of a watch like that, but the subframe lesson had been learned and I know I did the right thing. Didn't I?

6

The Long Walk to Austria

Summer was coming to an end, my relationship was coming to an end, I had no job and very little money. This was, conveniently enough, one of the main reasons my girlfriend was leaving me. After all, who could resist a rich man with a Porsche, his own business, and a nice house just doors away from the best pub in town? The fact that he was a lot older did not seem to matter, at least not in the beginning.

Rumour has it that I may have continued to see said girlfriend on the odd occasion when the new beau was out working. The downside of having all that money, as it turned out, was that you had to work hard to keep it, which theoretically presented an opportunity for an old flame to keep things smouldering a little longer than perhaps he should have done. When the cat's away, men and mice will play, and the leaves may or may not Russell.

There I was. No job, no money, and now no responsibilities. Winter was around the corner, which could have been thoroughly depressing, had I not hatched a plan with two of my old school friends, Chris and Andy, to work a winter season in Austria. Phil was not an option here, as things tended to go sideways whenever he was involved, and this venture needed to be spot on.

The next question was how three young men with limited resources were
going to get to Austria at the end of November. After many discussions, back and
forth on itineraries, and after much deliberation, we finally decided that we would
walk to Austria. By walk, of course, I actually mean hitchhike.

The day to leave arrived. We packed our backpacks with everything we
imagined we would need: sleeping bags, a small gas stove, many sets of thermal
underwear, gloves, hats, scarves, and in my case, a super bright neon ski jacket,
Nevica if memory serves. It was highly visible, which I convinced myself would
double up as a bright deterrent to any oncoming cars who would see us from
many miles away.

After our goodbyes and one last hearty meal, we were dropped off at the
junction of the M6 on the A5 in Cannock. It was mid-morning and we really did
not know what to expect. We were thankful with our first ride, all of us together,
I seem to remember we ended up at a service station just south of Birmingham.
Not far, I know, but it was our first lift, it was a success, but more importantly, we
had not been murdered and chopped into little pieces.

It was also very fortuitous, because this is where we secured what might go
down as one of the coolest hitchhiking experiences ever. Vintage, classic Jaguars
on their way to Munich, not just one, but three. We had one each. To this day
I am not entirely sure how we negotiated our passage to Munich. I imagine
it began with us admiring the cars, which, as you know, is one of my stronger
subjects. Whatever we said worked, because we were offered a ride all the way to
the ferry to Holland and then down through Holland into Germany.

The ferry was overnight, so we managed some upright sleep in highly
moulded plastic chairs, super uncomfortable, but free, which has always been my
favourite price. If I remember correctly there were two XJSs and one E-Type,
all soft tops, though it was mid-November so I doubt the roofs came down. I
honestly do not remember which car I was in, but I suspect it was one of the
XJSs, because I am fairly sure I would have remembered if it had been the
E-Type.

                    SIXTY NOT OUT

What I do remember is the attention we got on the Autobahn. It is not every day you see three classic sports cars, steering wheels on the wrong side, driving in convoy through central Germany. We received plenty of waves and horn beeps, and we felt rather spectacular.

We reached Munich in style, quite quickly and very cheaply. I think we only paid the price of a single foot passenger on the ferry. Things were looking up. The next step was simple enough. Find the Bahnhof in Munich and buy a one-way ticket to the promised land, which for us was Kitzbühel in Austria, a very reasonable two and a half hours away.

The men with the Jaguars kindly dropped us outside the station. It was already getting dark, so we headed straight inside to purchase our tickets. This is where we encountered problem number one. There were no trains to Austria until the following morning. Shiten.

We sat on benches in the station and tried to figure out what to do. We knew two things. We were hungry, and we had nowhere to sleep. The area around the station was a little sketchy, as is often the case in big cities. We could not afford, and did not particularly want, to stay in a hotel. They would have been dirty, seedy, and noisy, with those red lights glowing far too brightly for our liking.

What we could do, however, was take advantage of cheap as chips food. So we overindulged on various forms of potato and schnitzel until our bellies were full. Part one of the problem solved. Part two would be trickier.

Back in the station, it was dark, cold, and we were being told it was about to close. Staff would be locking up with iron gates and a padlock. Time to think outside the box. By now the station was super quiet, which suited our plan perfectly.

Just before the guard did his final sweep, we all, coincidentally, needed the toilet. It was quite a large one, and we each managed to secure a stall. The plan was simple. Stay in there until the guard had finished and left. The Bahnhof bogs, one star.

Over the tannoy we assumed they were announcing that the station would close in five minutes. It was all in German, but we distinctly heard funf and ende repeated several times, which we took as confirmation.

Our plan nearly fell apart when we realised the guard was checking the toilets. We heard him in the ladies next door. He shouted something in German, which I translated as, "Is there anyone in here?" No one responded, and we heard the lights switch off.

Footsteps grew louder as he made his way to the Herren. In perfect unison, like a badly rehearsed comedy sketch, all three of us lifted our feet and crouched on the toilet seats. The door opened, he shouted again, we stayed silent, and he switched the lights off.

Then, to our horror, we heard the click of the lock.

At the time, we thought we were safe. Now, as a sixty-year-old, all I can think about is fire, being trapped with no escape, and becoming infamous as the three crazy English boys who were barbecued in the Bahnhof bog. To make matters worse, we actually lit up our Calor Gas stove to keep warm, having moved from the stalls into the slightly more spacious sink area. It was more comfortable, but the smell was worse thanks to the uncleaned urinals.

It was a long night. The floor was dirty, hard, and freezing cold. The stove ran out of gas in the middle of the night, which was probably for the best. It remains the first and last time I have ever slept in a toilet. I would not recommend it. If you have a choice, take the red light hotel.

The toilets were unceremoniously unlocked around 6am. After one final crouch on the toilet lid, we stumbled back to the eatery from the night before, a little more disheveled, a lot stiffer, considerably smellier, and very hungry. Breakfast was glorious, the coffee was heavenly, and the warm air from the heater felt like a miracle.

Soon enough it was time to return to the station, not to sleep this time, but to catch a train. Kitzbühel, here we come.

Austria was a blast. Eventually. In the beginning it was tough and a little mundane.

My memory fails me slightly here, though I have a valid reason for that, which will emerge much later, in the early 1990s. For now, back to my first days in Kitzbühel. I cannot remember exactly where I stayed for the first week, probably some sort of hostel. Chris and Andy already had jobs and accommodation lined up at hotels, unlike me, who preferred to wing it.

While they worked, I wandered around town, cold and increasingly bored. Time to get a job. As in Ibiza, there was a strong sense of community among seasonal workers. Through word of mouth, or perhaps a notice on a bulletin board, I managed to line up an interview at one of the poshest hotels in town. I went in hoping to be hired as a barman or busboy. I came out as the newly appointed potato peeler. Mr Kartoffel to my friends.

This is where the mundane part of my trip truly began. I was expected to peel upwards of one hundred potatoes per shift, all by hand. My right wrist ached like never before, and never has since. Honest.

I lasted about ten days, or roughly one thousand potatoes in potato time. It did, however, serve a purpose. By some twist of fate, the hotel was directly opposite the best pub in town, The Londoner. After each shift I would cross the road to rehabilitate my wrist with exceptionally tasty local beer.

Time to introduce you to the man who would rescue me from potato hell, the one and only Rik Gunnell. Rik told me he had a job available as a gopher. Not entirely sure what that meant, I asked him. He gave me that wry smile, as if he could not believe I was walking straight into his trap, in his best cockney accent said, "If you work for me I'll tell you to go for this and go for that. You don't ask questions, you just fucking do it."

Job description delivered. I started the next day.

There was no formal training. I learned on the go. Each morning we travelled to three or four of Rik's other Londoner pubs, delivering alcohol and collecting money from managers. I also restocked merchandise, eventually Rik trusted me enough to drive the van alone, though not quite enough to handle the cash.

Within a couple of weeks my life had completely transformed. I lived in a company apartment with a group of Aussies, all barmen. I was the only Pom, and I took a bit of stick for it, though I suspect Rik's presence softened their teasing. I had my own transport, and best of all, free beer at the best après-ski bar in town. To top it off, the first big snowfall arrived. The season had officially begun.

Over the next few weeks I got to know Rik as well as anyone ever really could. He told me stories of his time in London, his life as a music promoter, and he claimed he had once managed Tom Jones. At the time I was not entirely sure I believed him, but later research suggests he was probably telling the truth.

More importantly, Rik taught me something fundamental. He showed me that it was acceptable to carve your own path, to live fully, to be respectful, but to enjoy life without apologising for it. Happiness, he believed, attracted opportunity.

Life settled into a brilliant rhythm. I worked in the mornings, skied most afternoons, and spent evenings either helping behind the bar or enjoying myself on the other side of it. I did not see much of Chris and Andy, as our schedules rarely aligned, but I had found my crowd among the ski reps who brought their clients to The Londoner. I even collected a prized selection of official rep sweatshirts, my favourite being a much-coveted La Piste sweatshirt from the Finnish company of the same name.

There were two notable mishaps that season. One was life-threatening, the other career-threatening.

Kitzbühel is home to the famous Hahnenkamm run, fast, dangerous, and for experienced skiers only. Whether Chris and I qualified as experienced is

SIXTY NOT OUT

debatable. After three or four weeks we had taught ourselves the basics, though our style left a lot to be desired. We could get from the top to the bottom quickly, which was all that mattered to us.

One late afternoon we decided to squeeze in a quick ski. We didn't check the weather, which was mistake number one. As we began our descent, the temperature dropped, the light faded, and the piste turned to sheet ice. Our edges could not grip, and turning became impossible. We skidded, fell, and flailed our way across the mountain before deciding to venture slightly off piste where the snow was softer.

For a while it worked, until we sank two feet into powder surrounded by trees. It was getting dark. By sheer luck, two cable car operators decided to ski down that evening and spotted us. They guided us safely off the mountain. I genuinely believe without them we might have had to spend the night up there, which we would not have survived.

That night our rescuers drank my entire beer allowance, and we gained a healthy respect for the mountain.

Christmas that year felt strange. It was my first time away from home, and my parents were separated. I felt deeply sad not to be with my mum, even though I knew she would have wanted me to enjoy myself. It was a difficult first.

New Year's Eve, however, was anything but quiet.

The Londoner was packed from late afternoon. By nine o'clock it was absolute chaos. Jaegermeister flowed, music blared, and everyone was drinking, including us behind the bar. At 11.50 the bouncers locked the front door so they could celebrate too, a questionable decision at best. Guess who ended up with the key.

Countdown came and went. People sang, danced, kissed, and celebrated. Then hundreds of them decided they wanted to leave. Rik asked me for the key. I could not find it. Panic set in. People pushed toward the door, the bouncers shouted, mainly at me, and things got ugly.

A decision was made to break the door open, not an easy job considering it's a fire door but eventually it was opened and a near disaster was averted. Rik was, as you can imagine, not too pleased but the fact that he had probably drunk twice as much as me meant his wrath was watered down and by the end of the night he even saw the funny side. Well that's what I'd like to think anyway. Perhaps he lived by the mantra of the last song we used to play every night, just as the lights were coming up. Always look on the bright side of life, da dum, da dum, da dum, da dum. Monty Python. Iconic.

To this day I have never disclosed this but two minutes later I discovered the key was still in my pocket, buried deep. To save face, I placed it discreetly on the floor behind the bar and announced that I had found it. Too late to save the door, but possibly just in time to save my job.

The next morning I had a brutal hangover and a meeting with Rik. To my relief, he accepted he should never have put that responsibility on me in the first place. He also hinted that he saw potential in me and would talk about future opportunities. Happy bloody New Year.

January brought more snow, more business, and more talk from Rik about staying on after the season. He even floated the idea of managing one of his bars, with a possible franchise in the future. It was one of those unexpected crossroads in life.

I was still young and inexperienced with life let alone life decisions so I probably didn't give it the attention the situation deserved, it's something that I occasionally wonder about now and if I had of said yes what would my life have looked like ?

In the end, my heart pulled me home. My parents were divorcing and my mum was struggling, despite her insistence that I live my life, I could not stay away. Rik understood and said there would always be a place for me if I changed my mind.

SIXTY NOT OUT

I returned from Austria more confident, more adventurous, and hungry to see the world. I also returned by plane, which was far less romantic than hitchhiking, but significantly faster.

Springtime in Wolverhampton arrived the same as springtime anywhere, full of new beginnings. I slipped back into the Birmingham modelling scene, doing work for Campri Skiwear that later appeared in Littlewoods stores. This led to an invitation to work their booth at the NEC, which sounded glamorous enough to tempt me.

The reality was standing around in ski gear under blazing lights, boiling hot, desperately waiting for lunch breaks when I could change into normal clothes.

It was on one of those lunch breaks that I met the woman who would become my third girlfriend, Amy.

7

Amy and the Far East Connection

On paper you would probably quite rightly come to the conclusion that Amy was perfect girlfriend material. Outgoing, adventurous, loved to travel, attractive and young. Now the young bit would eventually come back to bite me on the arse, but in the early days things were good.

I got on well with her dad who was a retired airline pilot. They lived together in a picturesque cottage by Halfpenny Green airport. She had unfortunately lost her mother just before I met her so it was just the two of them. She had two older sisters, one lived in London and the other in Singapore.

Being the daughter of a retired airline pilot came with benefits, namely cheap flights to anywhere in the world. After a summer of getting to know each other, and with both of us in the world of modelling, we decided to book a trip to see her sister in Singapore. We knew there was potential to do a little modelling on the side over there as they liked the "western" look, so we thought we had nothing to lose.

Amy was very familiar with Singapore as she had lived and schooled there for a while when she was younger, so I had a built-in tour guide. Her sister also lived in the most upmarket neighbourhood in a beautiful house, which we stayed at, so I was very fortunate. We had a fun time in the heat, and wow it was hot. Hot is bad, but hot and humid is the worst. I remember my first experience with air conditioning in a car, something that was not too widely used in Wolverhampton. I jumped in at the airport and straight away wound the window down, UK style, only to be shouted at by the cab driver that the AC was on and to wind it back up as quickly as I could. A mistake you only make once.

We regularly met up with a few of her old friends, drank cold beers and ate noodles at many of the hawker stalls at the night markets. One such school friend was Kay, whose family lived in one of Sydney's suburbs, and we were invited down to visit a week or so later. We had picked up a little work with some of the agencies and had a little spare cash, so we threw caution to the wind and bought some tickets to Down Under. Well, I bought tickets. Amy just put in a request to fly down there courtesy of her dad's ex-pilot perk.

We just did typical boyfriend and girlfriend stuff while we were in Oz. I scored contact details for a model agency in Sydney who were happy to put me on their books. I do not think I got any work from them on that trip, but it was a contact that would prove fruitful in the future.

Our first trip to Singapore and Australia seemed to be a success. We returned to the UK with the belief that we would return as soon as we could, as the potential and opportunities in Asia far outweighed anything we could achieve back in the UK. We wanted to travel and we could use modelling as a way to pay for it. Perfect plan.

A month or so later we were ready to go again. This time, after much research and faxing of pictures back and forth, we had also added Hong Kong and Taipei to our ticket, as these were hot markets for "gweilo's", Cantonese for Westerners. Look out Asia, here we come again.

Same set up in Singapore. The sister's fancy house, great hospitality from her and the affluent American husband at the time. The work was steady. We were both getting regular bookings. I tended to get more commercial looking jobs while Amy was more editorial. Everyone kept telling us to get to Hong Kong as soon as we could, as there was a lot of work there and it was a bigger market than Singapore.

We took everyone's advice and jumped on a plane a little earlier than planned and flew up to Hong Kong.

If you have never been to Hong Kong it is difficult to sum it up in a few sentences. We flew into the old Kai Tak airport in Kowloon, which was an experience in itself. Let's just say Hong Kong turned out to be my place. I can honestly pinpoint the moment that I landed there for the first time, that from that moment on my life would never be the same again. I truly was Made in Hong Kong.

The modelling set up was pretty similar to Singapore but multiplied by ten. Everything was ten times noisier, ten times more overcrowded and ten times busier on the work front. We had the ability to join as many model agencies as we wanted. There were many to choose from, but most westerners tended to stick to the same four. Models International, Cal-Carries, Da Silva and Irene's.

The secret to success in the modelling world is not all to do with how you look, but more importantly how you interact with your agents and subsequently how you interact with clients and photographers. I learned early on that if I could win over the agents and the team on the other side of the camera, then the battle was half won. Be punctual, be polite, be professional, always bring a decent selection of wardrobe if that is required, and most of all, do not complain.

Tools of the job included a portfolio of pictures, a comp card, which is basically a big shiny business card but much bigger showing your best four or five pictures, an A to Z of Hong Kong, an MTR card for the subway, and last but definitely not least a pager. Once a casting came in, all the agencies would scramble to connect with the models via their pager as it was always first come, first served. If Irene's models contacted me first about a casting, then if I booked the job it would go through them and they would earn the commission off the booking. Therefore it made sense for them to reach out to the models they thought had the best chance of booking the job. I was one of the lucky ones whose pager went off pretty frequently.

We settled into Hong Kong's frenetic pace without too much adjusting. Accommodation was small and very expensive, not to mention basic. The city woke up very early and went to bed very late. The noise, the smell and the sheer amount of people was overwhelming. The heat in the summer was intense, but it had a unique quality that was addictive. The local Chinese worked extremely hard and that work ethic was contagious. Whether it was a guy setting up his street butcher's shop, complete with flat ducks sweating and shining in the glare of the sun, dripping their fat all over the sidewalk while being naturally flavoured by the constant pollution of car fumes or dripping AC machines, to the small toothless guy on the corner happy to sell a couple of packs of cigarettes. Everyone was committed to work. Long hours and piercing heat were no match for the economic miracle that was Hong Kong.

As with everything in life there is a balance, a ying to the yang. So not only did we work hard, we also played hard.

There was a core group of friends that we had formed, made up of models from all nationalities and a group of Brit expats that shared our love of sarcasm. We would hang out regularly at the regular expat haunts, which were at the time, and probably still are now, Lan Kwai Fong and the bars in Wanchai. We would drink ourselves silly, dance with the most bizarre dance moves and in most cases find ourselves sitting in the gutter, greasy kebab in hand, mumbling about how fantastic our night had been. Our good friend Stuart summed it up perfectly when he called it "gutter time" because it was in fact time we spent in the gutter. I feel all fun evenings have to end somewhere, ours, on the majority of times, ended up there.

 SIXTY NOT OUT

Stuart was a very clever Oxford Uni grad who had established himself early on as a successful mover in the finance world of Hong Kong. With that he had all the trappings of a man doing well. A nice apartment, not small, dirty or noisy, and definitely not expensive for him, although I feel it was probably very expensive for his company. I feel his company was successful enough to cope however, as Stuart also had access to the company boat "Big Bill", on many a Sunday a big group of us would go out and visit all the local places that people with big boats went to. Stanley, Lantau Island or Shark Bay. It was always fun waterskiing or swimming in Shark Bay, very relaxing. Again, this usually turned into a great opportunity to drink, although we normally did not need a great opportunity. Just any opportunity would do.

The weeks rolled into months and the work kept rolling in. For the first time in my life I started to realise that I was onto something special, and for someone who had never had a pot to piss in, the possibilities of making some decent money were starting to become a real thing. I was actually in a position to start saving money, for the first time ever. So much so we decided to cash in our flights to Taiwan and concentrate just on Hong Kong, which from now on I am going to abbreviate to HK to save my typing fingers.

Just as my career was skyrocketing, Amy's probably started going the other way. Now I put that down to a number of factors. I was obsessed with work by now and would put that above my relationship at times. If there was a possibility I could get a job then I was going to get to that casting at all costs. I was requested more for auditions than Amy because she was blonde, and by the very nature of where we were there were not as many opportunities for blonde models, boys or girls. I have to be careful how I say this, but with my coarse spiky dark hair and almond shaped eyes I looked like I belonged in HK.

So where my work ethic was extreme, Amy was a much more chilled individual and did not have the desire I had to push myself to the limit. I felt like I was working and saving for our future. I was so wrapped up in that, I did not see the cracks starting to appear in our relationship, which was so blind of me because I really loved this girl and was starting to see and plan our life together.

In my mind she was my girl. In my mind she was going to be my wife one day. The trouble is it was all in my mind and I did not communicate it. For sure we had had the cutesy couple talks when you talk about life together, where would be a perfect place to live and so on and so forth, but I thought I had time. I thought I could keep saving and the unspoken bond that we had would keep getting stronger. Little did I know that the harder I worked, the more it weakened our relationship.

This is when that age gap started to manifest itself. We were on completely different trajectories. There was me, getting on a bit, contemplating settling down and working hard to build that nest egg, completely oblivious to my girlfriend's needs, who was having fun, travelling and being spoiled. I definitely took my eye off the ball when it came to spoiling her. I just wanted to save as much as possible for our future. Amy just wanted to have fun in her future.

It was inevitable the cracks were there. I chose not to see them. Maybe I was greedy, but for a boy that had found the goose that was laying multiple golden eggs, it was hard to classify it as greed, more of an opportunity, an opportunity that had to be capitalised on for as long as it was there, as it turned out it was there for a long time.

We had planned on returning to the UK for Christmas. We had separate flights as Amy's was a standby she had chosen to leave a week or so before me, not sure whether that was due to me staying longer to work or her desire to get away from me to give herself some space, which we had discussed and thought a good idea, and also a little time to "think". I am sure it was a combination of both.

We are talking about the Christmas of 1991 here. Faxes were still a thing, but it was way before cell phones. I mean cordless house phones were only just making an appearance. My point being that communication between loved ones was very challenging, not to mention the eight hour time difference.

SIXTY NOT OUT

Time to applaud my friend Stuart again, or more to the point Stuart's company. Technology was in its infancy here, but to enable Stuart's company to talk with their offices in London, there was a number you could put into your regular house phone before dialing the number you wanted, a code if you will. I do not profess to know how it worked, but by routing the call through his London office it turned out to be a completely free call, for as long as you wanted. That worked for me, well it would have done if I could have got hold of Amy. She was proving to be a little elusive.

My turn to fly back home came around, which was always an adventure. On most of my flights back to the UK over the years, especially on a 747, there were always multiple seats available, so after take off I would find a row of four, pop a sleeping tablet, eye mask on, giving out all those "do not disturb" vibes, and twelve hours later back into the cold, damp weather that was London in December. Quick shuffle over to the National Express bus stop just in time for my coach trip back to Wolverhampton, via numerous towns on the way, made all the better when accompanied by upbeat songs courtesy of my bright yellow Sony Walkman Sport. A nearly five hour journey which really should only take two and a half at a push, or three cassette tapes if you listen to both sides, which you could with the Sony Walkman Sport without having to take the tape out. Now there is some early technology for you right there.

Well it was not just the time difference or lack of technology that made it difficult for me to get hold of Amy from HK. I was having trouble getting hold of her once I was back in the UK.

I had heard rumours, and they were only rumours at this stage, that the space we had discussed giving each other had already been filled by another person, someone who was the complete opposite of me. I know that is how it normally works, but he was young and carefree. I guess I was old and boring. Ah well, maybe it was only a fling. I was in denial I suppose, but it looked and felt like my whole world was about to come tumbling down. I think we got together a couple of times to try to discuss it, but the writing was on the wall. I had been cast aside for a younger model, car reference not male model reference, and there was to be one humongous nail in the coffin which would leave me with no doubts.

The main social event of that Christmas was a huge party being thrown by MTV and Andy Taylor of Duran Duran fame. I was invited and so was Amy. In fact the invite was for us both as a couple. Apparently we had some sort of reputation as the model couple from HK, strange I know but true I guess. Unfortunately we were no longer a couple and I was now no longer in denial, in fact I was probably in the early stages of heartbreak, which I of course kept to myself. I had no intention of going to the party as I was not in a mood to party.

I remember staying in with my mum that night and consoling myself that I was being a good son by spending some quality time with my mum, who I knew struggled with heartbreak herself, especially at Christmas. As the night progressed I kept thinking about the party, so much so I convinced myself I had to drive over there to see for myself, and that is what I did. I do not think anyone ever knew that I did this. I would have been too embarrassed at the time to tell anyone. I never had any intention of going into the party. I mean I was not even dressed for it, but just rolled up to the lane outside, parked up for a while and sat there listening to a couple of songs I could hear in the distance beyond all the MTV trucks and lights, just imagining what it was like inside.

It was at that precise moment, the penny dropped and I realised that after more than three years together, Amy and I were done. A painful realization, but in reality she wanted something more than I could give her, and that was a fun filled free life, whereas all I had wanted was a life with her.

Time to get back to HK, back to things that I could control. Time to get back to work.

The first few weeks back were hard, returning to our apartment, discussing with friends what had happened, but I threw myself back into the world of HK modelling, something I was familiar with and something that gave me immense

SIXTY NOT OUT

pride. I surrounded myself with familiar faces and started to enjoy life again, started to enjoy life as a single man.

All the western models out there were one big family. I had friends from Canada, the US, Europe, Australia, and New Zealand. It really was a global melting pot. Socially I found myself hanging with the Aussies more than any other nationality, whether it was a reminder of the fun times I had had with their countrymen in Kitzbühel or whether I just loved the Aussie passion for life I am not sure, but whereas they were mainly male in Austria, the Aussies I hung out with in HK were predominantly female, female models at that.

It was strange how it worked out, but at work I found myself working with mainly models from the US, but socially it was all about the girls from Down Under. Now would probably seem like an appropriate time to tell you about a little dalliance I happened to have with one of my Australian friends, Kim. We were, and still are actually, really good friends although I have not seen her for a long time now.

I ended up being a bit of a jerk and quite insensitive as it turns out. We used to all go out in big groups, drink way too much and party real hard. I was aware that Kim liked me. She was super cool and younger than me, which I liked because it helped me stay young too, that is how I justified it anyway. I think my mind was still messed up from all the Amy stuff, but anyway we ended up together one night in some sort of drunken haze. I seem to remember me fumbling around a lot and not giving a good account of myself, if you get my drift.

The next morning was awkward as she lived in a house full of other models and I suspect they all knew what had gone on. There was one model there, an English fit model, not physically fit but fit in terms that he worked as a fitting model. He really liked Kim and saw me as a scoundrel and a rogue. I'm guessing he was just jealous in reality. Anyway, he got in her ear about me, but Kim and I managed to work our way through it and maintain a friendship, which does not happen often. If you leave the friend zone then it is normally very difficult to return to that friend zone, but return we did.

There is another dalliance to come, but you will have to wait a while until I spill the beans on that one.

Another one of the benefits of HK is its proximity to many other fabulous places, and the added benefit of modelling in HK is that you get sent to many of those fabulous places to work. You would think nothing of jumping on a plane to the likes of Bangkok, Kuala Lumpur, Manila, Taipei, Jakarta, Seoul and many cities in China.

I loved going to China. The southern cities of Shenzhen and Guangdong were easy to get to, as was Macau via the high speed ferry. Shanghai and Beijing were a breeze, but when you had to go to some of the more remote Chinese cities it got a little challenging, or shall we say downright dangerous.

On more than one occasion I have flown on old Tristars or DC-10's that should have been decommissioned many years ago. Smoking was still allowed on board and the nicotine stained fuselage and seats were testament to that, not to mention all the men in the back with crates of chickens on their laps. Safe flying this was not. Needless to say I survived and the cities I got to visit were well worth the stress of the plane ride.

In fact, flying in China is another level. On one occasion I had been working at a ribbon cutting ceremony for the brand Kindon that I was the face of. They were opening many stores throughout China and I had the opportunity to be a part of that tour. We had made many TV commercials in HK which had to be seen to be believed. Very cheesy, very over the top, lots of Rolls Royce's, helicopters, gold bars, just accurately portraying a normal day in the life of a western man. That is what we do every day right. Well that was the message they were passing onto your average Chinese citizen.

I was getting paid well, well enough to not have a conscience. I suppose, it proved successful as they had enough money to pay for me to travel over the country cutting ribbons.

I digress. The point of the story was that we ended up at one event later than we should have. I was due to catch the last flight out from the local airport and despite driving at 120 mph in a Mercedes that was at best two feet from the concrete median for over an hour, it was clear we were not going to catch that plane.

I do not claim to know the owner of the company well as there was a huge language barrier, but what I do know is that he was mega rich and mega connected. He managed, with one phone call, to delay the departure of the plane that had already left the gate. He got it to wait on the tarmac. We were allowed to bypass all security, drive straight onto the runway, they opened the door for me, wheeled up some stairs and I was able to stroll onto the plane, no boarding pass, and sit anywhere I wanted.

The guys at the back with the chickens were dumbstruck. I swear I saw one guy's cigarette fall out the corner of his mouth, a major fire hazard, but that was not going to bother me because I had been treated like a king and I felt invincible.

This turned out to be my life for the next few months. Playing hard, working hard, travelling and saving money. I was in a groove, life was ticking over perfectly again, healthy work, life balance. What could possibly go wrong now.

The answer was nothing. In fact things were about to get even better.

8

Introducing Miss Rowley

When I decided to live in Hong Kong indefinitely, I made a promise to my mum and myself: I'd come home twice a year. Christmas, and then again in June, when work slowed down a bit. I did it mainly for her, but also for me. Knowing a break was coming made it easier to push through the months in Hong Kong.

The first half of 1992 had been a mental slog, but by spring I was back to my usual pep. So, when June rolled around and I boarded the National Express after arriving from Hong Kong, I was genuinely excited. What mischief could a single man with a bit of spare time and a few bob get into? June 6th would prove to be significant. That was the day I met Vanessa, the young lady who would eventually become my wife, the mother of my children, and my partner in crime...all rolled into one.

Back in the UK, my circle of friends wasn't huge. Perhaps it was because I lived halfway across the world or maybe because I'm a touch aloof. I prefer the term "having lots of acquaintances." One such acquaintance was a well-known hairdresser-turned-bar-owner, let's call him Miguel. He called me one evening with a plan: a trip into Birmingham with his girlfriend and her best friend, and he needed a fourth. A free trip in an open-top red Ford Escort XR3? I didn't have to think twice.

Vanessa, my date and the driver for the night, was lovely...blonde hair and long legs, don't judge me, I knew they were long because the dress was very short so I just did the math.

She admitted she wasn't brilliant at parking, so I gallantly offered to help. It was an automatic, so steering and going forward were all she really needed to manage. I'd always had a thing for younger women, but ten years younger? I didn't expect anything romantic to come of it. Still, we hit it off. No expectations made it easy to be natural, and after parking her car, I joked that I'd already won her heart.

The club was our next stop: The Institute, partly owned by the same Andy Taylor whose party I'd missed six months earlier. Thanks to a web of connections, we were waved straight in. I even got invited into the VIP section, free drinks included, with some "extras" for good measure. Now, this was the early 90s, and ecstasy wasn't on my radar...until I found a little white pill in my hand. Jack Daniel's and Coke in one hand, E in the other, suddenly, a very uninhibited version of me emerged. I danced, laughed, talked nonsense, and became far more tactile than usual, focusing all my attention on Vanessa and her lovely long legs.

The night didn't end there. We returned to the Love Hotel, owned by Miguel's mum, Maureen. Whitmore Reans was not the safest place in Wolverhampton. I liked to call it White Maureen's as it was, in fact, owned by Miguel's mum who was called Maureen and she was, in fact, white.

We now get into sticky ground as we are talking about my future wife and the mother of my girls,all of whom are going to read my book, I hope, so I am going to give you two options of what happened next ... it's up to you to decide which is more likely.

             SIXTY NOT OUT

Option One. After bacon sandwiches and tea we settled down on the couch to watch two or three re runs of Fawlty Towers, my all time favorite comedy, I had watched it so many times that I could quote every line which really killed the vibe and contributed to Vanessa falling asleep on the couch, I gave her a peck on the head and headed back to my mums just as the sun was coming up.

Option 2. Soon after arriving back we learned that there was only one spare bedroom available, it was a single so it would have been a bit snug, I vaguely remember the decent side of me offering to stay on the couch but I think the naughty, tactile side of me had a way better argument that we share the single bed in a purely plutonic manner. The plutonic mumbo jumbo went out the window pretty quick and, once again but in a different context, Bob's your Uncle or more to the point, a bit of How's ya father!

By morning, which completely blows option 1 out the window, we shared a late breakfast and silently agreed we could have a good time together, even if it was just a summer fling. With six weeks until I returned to Hong Kong, that seemed plenty of time for a whirlwind romance.

That summer was unforgettable. Weekends at their holiday home in Abersoch, picnics on Wenlock Edge and more than picnics at Chillington Hall in Brewood, long walks with their spaniel, cooking together. It's possible I even started to win the parents over which is a biggie when playing the long game, I almost made a fool of myself at a posh restaurant once which could have derailed the whole romance, well to be honest I completely made a fool of myself but I somehow think it was all part of the magic that we were starting to create. I had ordered some sort of roast lamb concoction at Raymond Blanc's Le Manoir aux Quat'Saisons, it had been bound together with string which I inadvertently neglected to notice. As I took my first forkful, as only I could do I managed to swallow half the string and the other half got stuck in my windpipe - extremely embarrassing as I was conscious I wanted to make a strong impression with the parents, conscious I was in a super 5 star establishment and also extremely conscious that I might die! After rather uncouthly spitting out the food in my mouth, trying to remove the string with my fingers and gagging uncontrollably

I managed to remove the offending string just as everyone in the restaurant had turned to me to see what the bloody hell was going on! If the string didn't kill me then the embarrassment almost did. What an impression I must have made. I can't imagine what must have been going through Vanessa's dads mind looking at his possible future son in law coughing and spluttering all over the table, his hands in his mouth and his face turning a shade of red much darker than the glass of Chateau Margaux he was currently enjoying. It's fair to say I haven't been a big fan of lamb since that day.

We still found time to hit the clubbing scenes of Birmingham and my new favorite, The Hacienda in Manchester. Over the years we would visit the Hacienda many times but one occasion sticks in my mind more than any other.

We did the usual trip up the M6 from Wolverhampton after early drinks at the Light Bar, Miguel would normally drive his Renault 5, Vanessa and I would be crammed in the back, it was a fast little car and we would get there in no time.

As per Miguel's MO we would walk straight in, unfortunately his influence didn't stretch as far as getting free drinks but we were 80 miles from home so free entry was a bonus.

Now I don't see myself as a person with an addictive personality, I feel like I have enough self control to pick and choose when I want to drink or when I want to take drugs or, as on this occasion, do both. Tonight was a night I chose to do both.

Now if you ever went to the Hacienda in the late 80's or early 90's you would know how revolutionary and iconic it was, it truly was the place to be, it not only had its finger on the pulse of the acid house movement it was the pulse of the acid house movement, it was the home of house music and, in my humble opinion, home to the best DJ around - Graeme Park. Anyway enough of the commercial for the Hac, back to the night in question. Being a part time drug user I didn't have a clue about what was good and what was bad ecstasy, I knew you could end up buying a dud from some random guy you met in the toilets for twenty pounds and it didn't have enough MDNA in it to fire up an ant or you could buy one from another stranger and it be nearly pure MDNA and you would be flying for 12 hours. Big gamble. Crazy gamble. Looking back now a really crazy gamble. The only way I can rationalize it now is with the benefit of hindsight,the whole ethos of the club was built around drugs, gangs were allowed into the club for the sole purpose of selling drugs, it was big business and very lucrative. It was in their best interests to supply quality drugs that created the amazing atmosphere you always felt inside, that way the club would have longevity because it would remain popular, you get bad drugs in a place and people won't be back. The suppliers would set themselves up at the back of the stage and you really didn't want to have any direct contact with them … first of all they were armed and secondly they were scary.

Point of the rambling being I would always take half first to see what effect it had and if nothing happened then I would get another one and take that, as would sometimes happen, just as I had taken the second one the first half I took started to hit me. That was normally my limit - I don't think I ever did more than two in a night. Semi sensible I suppose.

I also had a little Whizz that night which is an amphetamine, the whole concoction made for a very uninhibited David. I would regularly dance on the podium or at the front of the stage, definitely not the back where the guns are. The best buzz you could get was all the energy the crowd got from you dancing and the energy you got back from the crowd, a mutual energy was shared and mixed with ecstasy, alcohol, a smidge of whizz and Graeme Park blasting out Searching … I got so in the zone that night I just didn't want it to end. I think we managed to get a few "one more" in by the time we had to leave. Rumor has it I was down to my underwear walking up the street outside the club once again asking random Mancunians where the after party was. I can neither confirm or deny this. I was bundled into the back of the Renault 5 quite unceremoniously as a half naked, high as a kite boy from Wolverhampton wouldn't have survived for too long on the Manchester streets.

Even now I can't remember how I ended up in my Calvins but the drugs that I had started taking back then was the main cause of my memory loss in later life. I still have selective memory loss if it suits my purpose but this is the real deal, I truly think the drugs I took in my late twenties are having an effect on my memory now at sixty.

One thing I do remember is that we went back to the Love Hotel and by now I probably don't have to give you two options of what happened there. All I can say is that we weren't watching Fawlty Towers.

Vanessa didn't seem to mind my little shows of exhibitionalism … she tolerated them and realized it was part and parcel of who I was. I think it was similar to modeling, I felt very comfortable with people looking at me, in fact I would go as far as to say I enjoyed it.

Time was ticking on and I would soon have to go back to HK. We were still inseparable so we decided to do one last crazy thing before I left … we would go to Paris.

We paired up with Miguel and Suzy again and headed over to spend a romantic few days in the city of love. It was such a fantastic time, whether it was taking romantic candlelit baths together in our quintessentially French hotel or rubbing shoulders, quite literally with Prince, Michael Hutchence of INXS or Helena Christensen at the ultra trendy, ultra chic Les Bains Douches nightclub. This was another one of Miguel's accomplishments - I don't know how he did it but he got us into the most exclusive club in the city and he didn't even speak a word of French. I must admit our girls looked amazing that night which probably helped but to get us in without paying yet again was Très impressionnant as they say in France.

I felt so blessed to be spending time with someone I had grown very fond of, it was a complete 180 of my relationship with Amy. I was no longer saving for my future, I was spending my money on someone who brought me a huge amount of happiness, someone that was happy to be with me for me and it was

SIXTY NOT OUT

all encapsulated within 3 or 4 wonderful days in Paris. This was the trip that really cemented our relationship and got me wondering how I would survive the next five months without seeing her. Decisions had to be made and they had to be made quickly, I mean, come on … I was falling in love with this lady.

It had been such an intense summer, full of excitement and new experiences but reality was just around the corner, well around the corner in HK to be exact, would our whirlwind romance stand the test of time and distance?

We were about to find out.

I pretty much fell straight back into work in HK. August was always a busy month and I found myself with lots of bookings. Vanessa and I talked regularly. It was decided that she would fly out to see me in September to spend a few weeks with me. After all the introductions and touristy visits to all the hot spots Vanessa naturally found herself hanging out more with the Aussies, like minded souls - far more fun loving than any other nationality, they were also closer to her age so it seemed only natural. As you remember from before I also like the Aussies.

Hong Kong was such a fantastic, cosmopolitan mix of nationalities all coming together and living in relative harmony. There were so many "expat" things to do. The downside, I suppose, was that you tended to see exactly the same people all the time. Whether it was the horse racing at Happy Valley on a Wednesday or Stanley Market on a Sunday, those familiar faces would pop up, the drinking would begin, and all hell would then let loose. Even if we were fortunate enough to go out on Stuart's company boat, Big Bill, it would start off all quite sensible but somehow end up in a drunken food fight at one of the restaurants on Lantau or Lamma Island. Very childish, but extremely funny. Annual events would get even wilder, like the HK Sevens rugby, which were epic with a capital E. Truly epic, I suppose. I also remember one evening when the England footballers were in town and they got some bad press because of the "dentist chair" fiasco in one of the local bars, Paul Gascoigne was the ringleader, now why doesn't that surprise me. Life didn't have to be all at 100 miles an hour all the time though,. there were plenty of places to just get away from it all, we particularly liked Shek-O where there was a tricky little coffee shop that had so many options of coffee bean all infused with different flavors that you could have ground on site either to take away or sit on the porch and drink long into those lazy Sunday mornings. Back on HK Island the Chili Club was also a fave, the most amazing Thai food. We went so often that when we rang up to reserve our table they knew who we were instantly. "Ahhh, Wooding." Don't get smart - I'm talking way before phone ID, and when we were there the waiter would always ask us if we wanted the usual. Sounds quite boring now, maybe we should have mixed the order up a little, gone a little spicier maybe, but I suppose once you find something you like you tend to stick to it, predictable doesn't have to equal boring, especially when it comes to Thai food. 701 with chicken and 706 with beef … can't be boring if I can still remember it over thirty years later. Wow, maybe my memory isn't too bad after all.

We managed to balance my workload with good times and, overall, the trip was a success. It also coincided with probably one of the busiest periods I had in all my time in HK - without blowing my own trumpet I was probably the most in demand male model and my work was insane. On some days I would have three jobs and two or three auditions that I had to do, but you know what … I loved it.

The mix of work was so eclectic that is what made it so enjoyable, in the morning I could be working in a dimly lit studio for David Hsiung shooting pyjamas and pants - English pants I might add, proper undercrackers. It pains me to say it but they were always super tight and cut really high on the leg … I'm happy to report the pictures were cropped and only showed my elongated trunk; just to clarify I'm talking about my midriff here; that was the only trunk on show. I know for years there was a polaroid somewhere in the house of one of these shots. I think Vanessa has it somewhere under lock and key should she need to blackmail me at any time in the future. I would get paid cash in hand for those jobs and would be on David's speed dial should a new shipment of pants drop unexpectedly. From pant to Pantene - I was also fortunate enough to get a lot of high paying gigs as well, one such job was Pantene.

We originally filmed in Manila for eight days. I was sailing yachts in Manila

Bay showing how the sea spray would damage your hair, we shot working out in a gym, swimming, anything that took a toll on your hair. The funny thing is they chose me for the job because they liked my face, strangely, I know but my hair color was too light so the first two days of the shoot was spent dying my hair jet black. I wouldn't normally allow them to do that because it was a semi permanent color and would take weeks to wash out and I would possibly miss out on more work. When they explained to me that they would in fact pay me to cover any lost work as well as very good money for the commercial itself then black haired David was happy to oblige. I also got to stay at the 5* Mandarin Oriental in Manila, all expenses paid which was a blessing in disguise as it was too dangerous to go outside after dark and anytime I went anywhere in the day I had to have a chaperone, it was in the days of the Marcos's and kidnapping of westerners was common. Yikes!

Luckily it all passed by without any issues and I was back in HK when a few weeks later, just as my hair was almost washed out, i got another call from Pantene to say they needed to do a couple of pick up shots and could I go to Bangkok this time for four days to shoot in a studio. You guessed it, the first two days they had to dye my hair back to match the original shoot, which took some doing. It proved difficult to match that Raven blue hue they had managed to capture at the original shoot in the Philippines. But, just as before, they were willing to compensate me enough that I was happy to be that guy walking around for a few weeks with what looked like a brooding Raven perched on my head. The haircut also seemed to mirror the bird's wings. I was the laughing stock for a while but it didn't bother me - I was laughing all the way to the bank. The Pantene job and a job I did for Toyota in Thailand were probably my best paying jobs, one of the most fun was shooting for Pepsi shoes with a successful local band called CC Riders - I was cast as the lead singer who had to dance on stage while lips syncing to their song " You make me Quiver" … I think my performance probably made them shiver! I remember shooting all night and the last shot was me falling to my knees with a close up from behind of the shoes, … it took a while but we got there. I must have impressed someone with the band because one time when Vanessa and I were in Bangkok they were also performing in the city and we got some backstage passes to go hang out during the show. Part of my inner ego hoped they might ask me to do a quick cameo but that wasn't to be, next best thing, however, they gave me a shout out and I got to wave at the crowd. Closest I ever got to being a rock God right there. As you can see I was blessed to have so much work but my next job did present me with a dilemma. I booked a fantastic job in Canada, Vancouver to be exact, for a shoe company, not Pepsi. Great money and a great experience, how could I not do it ?

I would be away for about six days but it was over the same time that Vanessa was supposed to fly home. What to do ?

Being a gentleman primarily and a guilt ridden boyfriend second I knew I had to make it up to her, I mean there was no way I wasn't taking the booking so I had to soften the blow. Vanessa had a close friend in Oman and it was arranged that we would buy her a new ticket back home via Oman, business class I might add, must have had too much money at the time or too much guilt of ending our vacation early, or a combination of both. Option three would be that she was upgraded by the airline. Now I'm a gentleman so I'm never going to tell, plus the fact that, yes you've guessed it - I actually cannot remember… bloody drug use taking its toll again !

Now Canada was an adventure. That is after they let me in. I spent about two hours in the immigration interview room as they suspected I was there to work, which I was. I didn't know that it would be a potential problem until I got a call from the crew in Canada just prior to me heading off to the airport. They had created a make believe scenario for me that I was meeting a friend of a friend from HK and they were going to show me around. I didn't have any money because they would pay for everything and they would meet me at the airport.

Simple story, stick to it and you'll be fine. It's a very different situation when a border guard is almost interrogating you, trying to catch you out. It's what they are trained to do, you know … I've seen it on TV !

Anyway, I channeled my inner "subframe" self and stuck to my story. It appears that at the same time they were questioning me they were also talking

SIXTY NOT OUT

to my "friend" on the Canadian side, lucky for us our stories matched up and I was able to enter. The highlight of the trip was my first real experience of North American coffee culture. Due to its close proximity to Seattle, Vancouver had a really cool place called Starbucks, not sure if you have heard of it, but it was still early days and I got my first experience of the tall, venti, grande conundrum. The job was great and I had less trouble leaving Canada than I did getting in.

Back in Hong Kong, work continued at a relentless pace. By the time December rolled around, it was time for my Christmas break, which was all about cementing our relationship.

Christmas in the UK was traditional chaos...log fires, pub lunches, old movies, tree on the car roof in the snow...but magical. I would say that Last Christmas by Wham was playing in the distance but that would be a stretch too far - the rest of it is true however.

Although I did get a black mark against my name on Christmas morning as I think, well I know that we over indulged on Christmas Eve and I kept my mum waiting until lunchtime Christmas Day before I eventually rolled home. I do have a good excuse however, well probably not a good one but an excuse nonetheless. It was all self induced intoxication. As was normal for me over this Christmas vacation that I was on, remember I'm in vacation mode and cannot be judged too harshly for my actions, I would partake in a few beers and a few recreational drugs. Now this may sound blasé but it was just good old fashioned fun. I'm strong minded and don't have an addictive personality so I knew I could control where and when I took drugs. Back in HK I never partook at all so I knew this was just a holiday blowout that I found exciting. Anyway on this particular occasion, Christmas Eve, I ended up actually going out under the influence. Vanessa's mum had some slimming tablets which we just happened to find and I knew, not from experience but word of mouth, that a couple of them would give you a bit of a buzz. Now Vanessa may or may not have partaken in a tablet as well, I'm not at liberty to either confirm or deny, it's her story to tell but I do remember both of us getting a fit of giggles just as we got in Vanessa's dads car with her sister who was driving us into Wolverhampton. It was a ridiculous decision to go out, it was so unbelievably foggy and icy that a journey that would normally take 35 minutes took well over an hour and a half, as luck would have, we were just passengers and Vanessa's sister was a much more accomplished and sober driver, she could even reverse and park which I know made her sister very jealous! It's a good job also as those driving skills were called into action as we hit a patch of black ice and we did a complete 360 that Torvill and Dean would be proud of.

Luckily for us by the time we came home the fog had cleared, we were also super starving so when we got back to Vanessa's parents home in the early hours of Christmas Day we ended up having a midnight feast, so much for the slimming tablets, I don't think they worked for me, well not in that capacity anyway.

If the Guinness Book of World Records had an entry for least amount of sleep on Christmas Eve then we would be in the running for it. I slept in the spare room when I stayed over at the house, it was still early days so we had to follow the rules of the house. Vanessa and her sister had their own rooms

Now if I tell you Jenny, Vanessa's mum, likes Christmas then that would be the under statement of the year... 5.00/5.30am was the norm ... now if you consider that our heads probably hit the pillow at about 4.50am then you will know without a shadow of a doubt that no more than 30 minutes later, heads still thumping, it was time for us to get up.

It was a long Christmas morning.

I eventually started to feel human again by mid morning, aided by numerous coffees and the sheer excitement of watching Vanessa open all her presents, I managed to peel myself away and went back to my mums to collect her as she had also been invited over for Christmas dinner.

Now my mum never got angry, well that's probably a lie, she never showed that she was angry, it always manifested itself in a more somber emotion ... more of a sadness or disappointment that had come because of the anger. She hid the

SIXTY NOT OUT

anger and showed sadness in its place.

Christmas morning was one of those times.

She was still at heart a creature of habit, when my parents were together we always had the traditional Christmas morning, presents at the bottom of the bed in pillowcases and the main ones under the tree downstairs. My brother and I had tried to keep that alive after the divorce and, with the occasional exception we probably succeeded.

It was something magical from the past she could hold onto. This was the first time she had spent Christmas morning all alone. I felt shitty.

I had let her down.

I wish I could say I made it up to her on New Years Eve but that would be a lie, I know we went out and partied hard, the only difference this time was that my mum wasn't expecting me back the next morning therefore I wouldn't let her down, I also doubled down with the explanation that it wasn't wise to drive if we had been drinking so we would stay over at the Love Hotel for good measure.

It was all fluff, it didn't really take away from the underlying sadness that I knew my mum would be on her own seeing in the new year - in fact I knew she wouldn't even be awake to see in the new year as she would go to bed way before 12.00 came around. Not a great place to be on New Year - on your own.

Little did I know that my New Years Eve guilt would pale into insignificance compared to the tragic events back in HK as I learned about the terrible events in Lan Kwai Fong, a place I frequented on a weekly basis and would almost certainly have been there had I not come back to the UK, for so many young people to lose their lives was beyond heartbreaking and completely unimaginable.

It was time for me to return.

Soon after my New Year hangover had gone it was time to hit the National

Express back to Heathrow, but now I had two people waving me off from Pipers Row coach station, my mum and Vanessa, twice the love but twice the sadness of leaving. I was slightly cheered by the strong bond they were forming and Vanessa's commitment to spend time with my mum while I was away - which she followed through on. I always remember I was pretty upset on the coach until I got to about Coventry but then either the tunes from my Walkman or the thought of going back to HK raised my spirits and I tuned into Rik Gunnell's philosophy for life and I always looked on the bright side of it.

As it happened Vanessa and I had fallen into a comfortable little routine, three months apart followed by two or three intense weeks together and our next meeting was to coincide with her 19th birthday in early April. Let me just pinch myself here … was she really only 18 ???

My three months of work were chaotic, in a positive way … lots and lots of bookings and, time to blow my own trumpet again, although it's something that I rarely do I have to admit that I was now the main western guy in HK, my picture was all over the subway, I was on lots of TV commercials, I did most of the high end advertising for the bigger labels and I even had a music show on TV - I sucked at this however, very scripted, every word had to be exactly as written as English language TV in HK was highly censored, I felt like a robot and struggled with the rigidity of it, I'm much more ad lib and unfortunately ad lib was a big No No. It turned out the second season was a No No too.

Apart from that I was crushing it, it even got to the stage that I used to get recognized around town which I guess is a big thing considering HK had a population of about six million.

Now I used to work with quite a few different female models both in HK or if we were sent abroad for a job. There was a group of maybe 12 of us, six boys and six girls, we would always go to the same auditions and basically compete against each other to see who got the job. Now bear in mind all the smaller jobs usually didn't have a casting - we were just booked directly. It was all the big paying, prestigious jobs that had castings and these are the ones you wanted to

SIXTY NOT OUT

get. I got more than my fair share on the male side and it was becoming more and more clearer on the female side that one girl was starting to get all the female jobs, her name was Stacie, I started to work with Stacie on a regular basis.

Time flew, it always does when you're busy and you have something exciting to look forward to, before I knew it we were a couple of days out from when Vanessa would fly back out.

Boracay

On this visit, it was my intention to dedicate more quality time and do more one-on-one things together. With that in mind, I booked us a trip over to Boracay in the Philippines. We had heard amazing things about it and were desperate to check it out.

It was not easy to get there. A couple of flights followed by a choppy boat ride made sure of that. I suppose if it had been easy, then every Tom, Dick and Harry would go, and it would not have remained the secluded, unspoiled paradise that it most definitely was.

Our accommodation was a basic hut, which was perfectly acceptable given that we were using Hong Kong as our benchmark. It was clean and had everything we needed, including a vast and deeply unwelcome collection of insects and bugs. That part took some adjusting to. Add in strange animal noises throughout the night and it made for a few interesting and largely sleepless evenings. Our cuddle ratio went way up on that trip, more for safety than passion, but I was happy to take a cuddle regardless of the reason.

The outside shower was another experience entirely. I was placed on guard duty every time Vanessa wanted to wash, tasked with keeping an eye out for any unwanted four-legged visitors. In truth, she probably should have been more concerned about the prying eyes of her two-legged boyfriend.

Or worse still, the prying eyes of a young local lad we spotted one evening peering through our window while we were in the middle of one of those "cuddles." I am not sure who was more surprised, him or us. I was also acutely aware that if I disengaged from our cuddle to chase after him, I might shock him even more. There was also the small matter of tripping, potentially pole-vaulting out of the window, and creating a far more dramatic scene than anyone needed.

I have been trying to use that joke for over forty years now since I first heard it. I cannot remember which comedian it came from, but if ever there was a moment for it, that was it.

There were a few homesick tears as well. It was the first time Vanessa had spent her birthday away from her family, and with no shops on the island I was at a complete loss when it came to buying extra gifts. Apart from what I had brought with me, and of course the main present, the trip itself, there was not much I could do. My hope was that a birthday full of memories would make up for the lack of wrapping paper.

Just off the beach there was a small shack. Calling it a café would be giving it ideas above its station. We went there every afternoon for banana cake, mango juice, and our daily backgammon competition. This was the most strenuous thing we did all day. Our mornings were spent on the beach, swimming in the most aqua-blue sea I had ever seen up to that point. We would doze in hammocks, then wander up to the shack later in the afternoon.

Exhausting, let me tell you.

On one such wander, it felt like we had stepped onto a film set, though not for the reasons you might be imagining. Please remove *Blue Lagoon* from your mind immediately. Just off one of the tropical trails stood seven or eight men dressed

SIXTY NOT OUT

in army fatigues, holding what I would have confidently referred to at the time as machine guns.

I have no idea why we did it, but we simply carried on walking. Straight past them. Straight to the shack.

At the time, we did not register the danger. In fact, I am not even sure there was any danger. The man serving our banana cake later told us they were there to keep the island safe. On a previous work trip to the Philippines, I had been warned not to travel a certain route after about four in the afternoon as it was patrolled by guerrillas. People had been kidnapped there, particularly wealthy westerners, and ransomed for money.

I do not pretend to understand the politics of the Philippines, but I suspect the men on Boracay were connected to something similar. Either way, we did not see them again, which came as a relief.

The threat of kidnapping in the region was very real. Later, while working in Manila for Pantene, I was not allowed outside the hotel for the entire week unless accompanied. Walking anywhere was not permitted. Hotel cars only. Given that I was staying at the Mandarin Oriental, it was hardly a hardship.

Unfortunately, a friend of mine paid the ultimate price the following year. He was kidnapped with two others in Cambodia while travelling on a road they probably should not have been on. The dangers were not theoretical. They were real, they were unforgiving. He was genuinely a good guy and a talented young model with a real thirst for adventure. I think about him from time to time. May he rest in peace.

There is, however, only so much banana cake, mango juice, backgammon, and paradise one can take.

Eventually, it was back to Hong Kong for me, and after a brief stopover, back to the UK for Vanessa.

Throughout her back-and-forth trips to Hong Kong, Vanessa had also been studying at the Montessori Academy in London. By the summer, she had graduated. Given our shared fondness for throwing caution to the wind, we decided it would be exciting if she moved to Hong Kong after the summer and took a job at the Montessori school in Repulse Bay.

Repulse Bay, for context, is a very swanky part of the island.

She got the job. We got a new apartment together. The building itself was scruffy, though the unit was cleaner and relatively modern. The phrase "lipstick on a pig" springs to mind, as it turns out. Still, we were gung ho. Let us roll the dice and see what happens.

After all, we had been together for a year. Seventeen weeks of that had been spent together in the same place, so more like four months in practical terms, but we felt we had achieved something.

Let the good times roll.

And roll they did, straight out the door.

This was a tough period. I do not think I was ready to fully commit to living with someone twenty-four hours a day. My lack of understanding and compassion for a young woman who had travelled halfway around the world to build a life with me was staggering.

Even now, looking back, it upsets me. I did not recognise the hurt I was causing. In my mind, I was still living my best life, making no effort to adapt to the reality of sharing it. It is no wonder things started to unravel.

There was another factor at play as well. Calling it dalliance number two would be wildly misleading.

This was me being unfaithful.

SIXTY NOT OUT

10

A Dalliance Too Far

So here's some context. I'm not trying to lay a foundation for some sort of pity party here. It was one hundred percent my fault and I take complete ownership. I was a weak-willed male who got swept up in the excitement of something that might have been. Instead of jumping off the bus at the first stop, I pretty much rode it all the way back to the terminal.

It was a journey that, in retrospect, was essential for me to take. It forced me to address some hard realities and make some tough decisions. If it hadn't happened then Vanessa would never have left HK, which in turn forced me to look within myself and ask the question I had been avoiding for far too long. What do I really want?

I digress. How did it all start? Well, as I mentioned before, I found myself working more and more with a model called Stacie. That was her modelling name, not her real name. She was a bit of a socialite, from a very wealthy family. A lot of people found her aloof, but I got on well with her and we worked well together.

Now when people start getting in your ear about how well you work together, how you always book jobs together, how you would make a nice couple, it starts to plant a seed. I'm not saying anything happened because of that, but when friends and work colleagues had been saying all this stuff even before Vanessa was on the scene, and even back to the Amy days, that seed started to grow a little.

The only logical way I can make sense of it is with the benefit of hindsight. At the time you're making decisions in the heat of the moment, and we all know how that goes. Looking back now, I can see that I probably felt trapped within my living conditions, which in turn led to friction in my relationship with Vanessa, which ultimately led me to stray. Easy to say now with a lot of water under the bridge, but at the time it was messy and confusing. It also carried a distinct sense of excitement.

It all came to a head in Saigon when we were shooting for the Omni hotel chain. We had been away on work trips many times before where there would have been opportunity, but nothing ever happened. We just carried on as friends. I remember one cool job we did in Thailand for Toyota where we were together for over a week, but again nothing happened.

All of those fantastic jobs we were doing together, in fantastic locations, for fantastic money, were little pieces of a jigsaw coming together. It felt like we were living in a make-believe parallel universe of glitz and glamour. I suppose we thought we were those people. There was an inevitability about it. Once all the pieces were in place, the only thing left was to go to the next level, which happened in Vietnam.

I tried to carry on as normal back in HK, but when I say Vanessa has a sixth sense I am not exaggerating. That girl was onto me like wildfire. Not long after we returned from Vietnam we had been to a murder mystery night at Stacie's apartment on the Peak. There I was, cheating, while still trying to keep two people happy. I was such a jerk.

     SIXTY NOT OUT

Stacie was understandably unhappy that I came to the party with Vanessa, and as we left she asked me to call her when I got home. In those days the only way to secretly call her was to sneak up to the 7-11 up the road and use the payphone. I remember making up some pathetic excuse about craving marshmallows and heading out.

I was halfway through explaining to Stacie that I couldn't come back to her place when I looked up and saw Vanessa standing in the doorway. I was busted. I deserved to be busted, and everything I was about to go through was self-inflicted and completely justifiable.

That was the start of the end of our life together in HK. Vanessa moved out and went to stay with the Aussies for a while, I just wallowed. I found little comfort in work, but it was the only thing I could cling to. Stacie wanted a relationship, but I wasn't sure that was what I wanted. Vanessa didn't want a relationship, and I came to realize, that was exactly what I wanted.

It was confusing. I was confused. I was an idiot. It was all my own fault, and now I had to make a decision. Should I listen to my heart or follow my head? Decisions and I have never gone well together, and I stumbled around for weeks trying to work out what I wanted.

By now I had moved out to stay with our friend Stuart so Vanessa could move back into the flat. She had just returned from a trip to Thailand with the Aussies, who were quite rightly telling her to move on from me as I was no good. There were also plenty of ulterior motives at play, as I knew a lot of the boys were keen to fill my shoes.

I remember one moment particularly clearly. We passed through the apartment, living our separate lives. She looked amazing, all tanned and glowing. She had prepared some food and asked me to stay for a bit and chat. For reasons I still struggle to understand, I rejected the invitation. Maybe it was an olive branch, maybe not, but I was rude and I left. She later told me how upsetting that was, even now thinking about it turns my stomach. How could I have been so cold?

I felt like I was living in no man's land for a week or so. I knew a decision had to be made for everyone's sanity, and as fate would have it, the decision was made for me.

Plumbing in HK was sketchy at the best of times, and if you combine that with the plumbing in an apartment I could afford, it was only a matter of time before the proverbial mess hit the fan. In this case, it backed up and flooded the entire bathroom.

That was the straw that broke the camel's back for Vanessa. She had kept her parents up to date with our situation and they were understandably concerned for their daughter. Add a full-scale plumbing disaster to the mix and there was really only one solution. Time to leave. Out came Dad's Amex and a ticket back to the UK was booked.

The decision was made. Vanessa was going back, she asked me not to contact her for two weeks to give me time to sort myself out. And I'm not talking about the plumbing. I remember being very choked up at the airport as the reality of my behaviour finally sank in. The only reason she was leaving was because of me. I had promised her parents I would take care of her and look after her, I had failed miserably on both counts. I was deeply disappointed in myself.

It was the last chance saloon, at least where Vanessa was concerned. The clock was ticking. Which proverb would prevail? Absence makes the heart grow fonder, or out of sight, out of mind?

I leaned heavily into the out of sight option and spent more time with Stacie. I remember having dinner with her parents once. It felt more akin to a job interview than a meal. I was constantly talking myself up because I didn't feel worthy as a mere model. We met her brother and sister one evening in Lan Kwai

          SIXTY NOT OUT

Fong and they were both lovely, but I had a nagging feeling that I didn't belong. More importantly, I knew I wasn't their kind of person.

We even discussed the possibility of them helping me find a corporate job through contacts in New York. My future was being mapped out for me and I had no control. If I were to have a future with Stacie, I would have to be moulded into someone acceptable to her family. I understood they only wanted what was best for their daughter, and I probably could have adapted, but it would have been a complete one-eighty for me. This wasn't just about being with her. It was about keeping an entire family happy.

Knowing that her mother also had grand designs on her ending up with a famous golfer, which she made no secret of, sealed it for me. I knew right there that this wasn't the road I wanted to go down. It may have worked for a while, but it was always destined that she would end up with the golfer and I would become collateral damage.

I found myself thinking about Vanessa more and more, and that became obvious. One night at a bar called California in Lan Kwai Fong, I was distant with Stacie and tried to explain that I was confused and missing Vanessa. She felt me slipping away and gave me an ultimatum. Choose.

I don't remember saying anything, but my silence was enough. I don't think I ever had another meaningful conversation with her. Who knows what would have happened if I had rolled the dice? But as I did in Kitzbühel, I followed my heart, not my head, once again it proved to be the right choice. It led me to the life I have now.

I haven't had contact with Stacie for over thirty years, but I know she eventually ended up with the famous golfer. I'm sure there were plenty of eligible fish in the sea for her before the shark swam in. As far as I can tell, she is LIV-ing happily ever after.

As the two weeks passed and the realisation that my heart belonged to Vanessa became undeniable, I found myself reminiscing about our time in HK. One memory that kept resurfacing involved Stacie as well. We had travelled to Bangkok for follow-up shots for the Toyota commercial, and I had asked Vanessa to come along as our friend Paulette was also there.

One day I had to do solo shots, and Stacie invited Vanessa to lunch while I was working. I think she wanted to assess what she saw as competition. I carried on with work and met Vanessa afterwards, only to hear how uncomfortable the lunch had been. I had been naive enough to think it was casual, unaware of the undercurrents at play.

If that lunch was awkward, time with Aussie Paulette was the complete opposite. High energy, fun, and completely unpredictable. If you know Bangkok, you'll know Patpong night market. Everything and anything goes there. On that particular night we stopped at a pharmacy and bought some over-the-counter slimming tablets. We didn't need to lose weight, just lose our minds.

We wandered through stalls selling everything from electronics to fake Ralph Lauren and mouldy durian fruit, the smelliest thing on earth. On the other side were strip bars and adult entertainment, with each floor getting racier the higher up you went. I never made it above floor two.

As we reached the end and started to circle back, we quite literally dodged a bullet. A guy on a scooter screeched up, pulled out a handgun, and started firing. It wasn't until locals began shouting and diving for cover that we realised what was happening. Slightly impaired or not, by the third shot we were flat on the floor behind an overturned table. I remember instinctively shielding Vanessa with my body. As quickly as it started, it ended. We jumped into a tuk-tuk and got back to the hotel, hearts pounding.

Memories like that cemented what I already knew. Vanessa was the one. True to my word, I waited two weeks and, with the help of Stuart's phone trick, I called at two weeks plus one hour.

     SIXTY NOT OUT

She wasn't in.

Had she moved on, or was she playing hard to get? It turned out to be the latter. She was away in Abersoch with friends. After swallowing a bit of humble pie with her mum, I reached her there.

She was cool, and not just because of the Welsh weather. I deserved that. I was prepared to do whatever it took to prove myself. It would take time and effort, but she was worth it. I knew I had found my forever person.

A three-week road trip through Europe in my Peugeot 205 Convertible forced the conversations we needed to have. I came up with this hair brained scheme to drive around Europe with no real plan and just stopping wherever we wanted or wherever took our fancy. The rough route was down through the west of France, through Andorra into North East Spain and then back around the South of France, a quick detour to Monte Carlo then into Switzerland and back home via Paris. There was no way we were not going to talk about my dalliance on that trip and there was no way for me to escape. I was quite literally in the hot seat! We had serious conversations but we also had so much fun, from pictures and picnics in Sunflower fields to our impromptu 1,000 mile parties, we even got into a little mischief in Sitges.

Out of character for either of us, we ran off without paying our restaurant tab. It was completely justified as we had asked for the bill repeatedly for more than 20 minutes. We noticed our server had clocked out and left . So we did, too. We planned it meticulously, we had to be calm and confident as we vacated our table so as to not draw any suspicion. We planned not to run until we were out of sight of the restaurant but that went out the window five steps from the front door. We both bolted while laughing uncontrollably so much that we didn't pay any attention to where we were going. After inadvertently turning right on three occasions amongst all the laughter we found ourselves passing the restaurant again! Crazy headless chickens, but more importantly we were two crazy headless chickens that knew they were meant for each other. We knew that our love was back on track.

I knew I had to leave HK, all the memories, all the adventures, the good times and the bad times and everything in between. It had served me well. Quite well. It was the catalyst to what was to lie ahead, I was able to take the money I had saved and invest in my future, or should that be our future. Change was coming. I will be forever grateful to HK for giving me the financial independence to take the next step.

In my mind, as I have said before, I truly was Made in Hong Kong.

- 11 -

The Proposal Down Under

If someone were to ask you to pick a country that was the complete polar opposite of Hong Kong, then Wales would probably be very high up on that list. For all the skyscrapers and office buildings, we now had sprawling farms and small hamlets. For all the millions of people, we now had millions of sheep and only a small fraction of the population. For all the noise and pollution in HK, we now had silence, the occasional tractor horn, and fresh south westerly winds bringing a whole host of weather.

Welcome to Abersoch in northern Wales. A quaint coastal village for most of the year, and a playground for England's wealthy and privileged during the summer months, with a few extra sporadic holiday weeks squeezed in between Easter and late October.

I was a relative newcomer to this beautiful village on the Llŷn Peninsula, introduced to it by Vanessa in 1992. We stayed at her family's holiday home, which had been in their possession for a few years before I arrived on the scene. It would later become the bolt hole we used on our return from HK, well, my return, and the place where we tried to repair our broken relationship.

I also thought that a nice trip to sun kissed Turkey might help. It was just the two of us and we wanted to get away, almost to find neutral ground that might give us the space and confidence to talk about where I went wrong. I think it worked. I know it helped. Between rolling around in the warm mud springs at Pamukkale and taking evening walks along the beach at sunset, we started to repair the damage I had caused. It was a small step, but we were finally heading in the right direction.

I knew that time alone was exactly what we needed. Vanessa is a talker. I'm not. But I also knew that if I wanted to save our relationship, I had to open up and talk. So open up and talk I did.

By the autumn of 1994 we were coming down to Abersoch regularly, spending hours walking on the beach, cooking, going to the local pub, and slowly becoming familiar faces in this close knit Welsh community. It worked. We felt ourselves falling back in love all over again.

Through everything, we had always loved each other. What I questioned, because of my cheating, was whether I was still in love. I certainly did not expect Vanessa to be in love with me after everything I had put her through. That said, we used the foundation of our love to rebuild something stronger than what we had before, something that far surpassed anything I could have imagined.

Once I managed to let go of the guilt, I could focus completely on the person I knew I wanted to spend the rest of my life with. I had been given a second chance and I was determined to repay that faith with all of me, forevermore. I know that sounds a bit extreme, but people say when you know, you know. And I knew.

We were properly back on track. The clarity and purity of the Welsh air had worked its magic. I was still in touch with my agents in HK, and when a well paid job came up in Kuala Lumpur it gave us the opportunity to put together a nice little trip. A quick stopover in HK, then on to Australia to see a few friends.

　　　SIXTY NOT OUT

This is where having a friend like Stuart once again came into its own. Not only was he the guy who facilitated those free phone calls back to the UK, but he also had a company apartment in HK that he was happy to share with friends. I counted myself grateful to be one of them. Accommodation sorted.

As you probably know, there are certain people in life you just click with. Vanessa was my person. We laughed at the same things, and on many occasions we would have exactly the same random thought at exactly the same time, however ridiculous that thought might be.

Such was the case during our stay at Stuart's. I had just finished telling Vanessa a particularly grim story about how my dad once put his big toenail into our cornflake packet and tried to pass it off as an actual cornflake. Don't ask me. I have no words. To make it worse, I'm not sure whether he painted the nail yellow or orange to match the flakes, or whether it was already that colour when it fell off. I'm guessing the latter, because healthy nails don't usually just drop off. Either way, it put me off cornflakes for a very, very long time.

At exactly the same time, Vanessa and I decided it would be hilarious to recreate the prank on Stuart. Unfortunately, neither of us had a suitably sized nail, and more importantly, Stuart didn't even eat cornflakes. He did, however, eat muesli every morning, back when muesli was a thing.

The plan was simple. Add a small, clean fingernail to one of the raisins and tell him about it before he eats it. What actually happened is a little fuzzy, but as I remember it, after carefully placing the doctored raisin at the top of the packet, Stuart announced he was running late and heading out for breakfast.

At that point we realised the prank had gone too far and decided to remove the raisin. Unfortunately, in doing so we knocked the packet and the offending raisin disappeared into the depths of the muesli, never to be seen again.

The right thing to do would have been to throw the packet away and replace it. For reasons beyond comprehension, we didn't. And when I say "we", I really mean me. After much laughter, the packet went back into the cupboard. Who isn't guilty of biting their own nails occasionally? I just wouldn't choose to eat someone else's.

I genuinely think we forgot about it. And how do you even begin a conversation like that? "Morning Stuart, slight issue with your breakfast." You don't. Profound apologies, Stuart. If I had to explain myself in a court of law, I'd still have no defence. Youthful stupidity, I suppose.

Anyway, back to some semblance of normality. The HK trip gave me the chance to lay a few demons to rest and prove my faithfulness. You are never going to guess who the job in Malaysia was with. I'll give you one guess. Yes. Stacie.

Looking back now, this is one of those moments where you realise just how impactful Vanessa's choices were. I went to her and said that if she didn't want me to go, I would completely understand and would turn the job down without hesitation.

I'd guess that seventy five percent of girlfriends would have said absolutely not.

Not Vanessa. She played it differently. By trusting me, she allowed me to prove to myself that I was trustworthy. She wasn't intimidated by Stacie, and more importantly, she knew I had chosen her. In simple terms, she had won. There was no way on earth I was going to betray that trust.

As luck would have it, I barely saw Stacie on the trip. She flew in earlier and did most of her shooting before I arrived. Our paths crossed briefly on my first morning for a few shots. I was polite and professional, finished the job, and went straight to the airport to fly back to HK. We were on the same flight but checked in and sat separately.

Vanessa was waiting for me at Kai Tak, and I knew Stacie would exit the plane ahead of me. This is where karma, fate, or a come to Jesus moment played its part. Vanessa positioned herself in full view as passengers came down the ramp. She only wanted one person to see her, and she made sure she did. No words were exchanged. Just a victorious little smirk. Vanessa is clever like that.

     SIXTY NOT OUT

By now, I was completely convinced. We spent a few extra days in HK enjoying ourselves, I fitted in a couple of small modelling jobs. But there was one important thing I had to do before Australia. I needed to visit a jeweler and buy a very special ring.

When a relationship progresses and you start talking about baby names, you realise you've found your person. Vanessa dropped plenty of hints, and I listened. She liked emerald cut stones, aquamarine, diamonds, and platinum. Finding a ring that ticked all the boxes was surprisingly easy. The moment I saw it, I knew.

Buying it was simple. Hiding it for the next four or five weeks was not. I knew I wanted to propose on Valentine's Day in Melbourne, but the details would come later. Transporting the ring was its own adventure. Checked luggage felt risky. Carry on felt even worse. I went with a combination of pocket and hand luggage, keeping it in the velvet box, which earned me a few sideways glances. Hands in pockets became my go to move.

Here's another one of those may or may not have happened moments on the plane ride down to Australia. There is an exclusive club that you can join if you are flying a certain distance above the ground and you perform a certain act … it's possible that we performed that certain act at the correct distance above the ground. Say no more.

We arrived in Sydney and stayed with our friend Kim, the same Kim I'd had a dalliance with years earlier. She had forgiven me. Vanessa had too. Kim's boyfriend had not. Strange bloke, but he did make exceptional lamb chops.

We did the Sydney highlights, then Melbourne. It was around the Australian Open tennis, so the city was buzzing. We drove the Great Ocean Road, visited Bells Beach, and even Ramsey Street from Neighbours. I once had ambitions of appearing on Neighbours as an extra. It never happened. The closest I got was wearing a pair of Jason Donovan's boots. I digress.

Australia Day came and went. February arrived. The clock was ticking.

On Valentine's Day, in Melbourne's Botanical Gardens, Romeo and Juliet was being performed on an open air stage. That was it. Picnic. Champagne. Ring in pocket. Hands in pockets. Front row seats.

By the interval, most of the champagne was gone. Dutch courage engaged. I asked Vanessa to join me on stage, dropped to one knee, and proposed in front of the remaining audience. She said yes. The ring fit. There was applause, hugs, kisses, and a slightly theatrical exit as I waved to the audience.

We were engaged.

There was just one small detail I had overlooked. I hadn't asked her dad.

We called her parents immediately. I apologised to her father and asked for his permission after the fact. He agreed, thankfully. Because of the time difference, it was still Valentine's morning in the UK, so technically it was still before I had proposed.

And that, according to my entirely flawless logic, means I followed etiquette perfectly.

Wales – Land of My Daughters

Soon it was time to pack up and head home to the UK. We had a future to plan and a marriage to arrange.

After we had overcome our jet lag from the imaginary time difference that we all now know doesn't exist, we were immediately bombarded with congratulations. Between Vanessa's mum's excitement and the fact my dad worked for the local newspaper, we somehow found ourselves interviewed and splashed across the front page of the *Shropshire Star*, complete with the full romantic engagement story for all to see.

Coincidently, we escaped to Wales the very day we knew it was being published, keen to avoid any unnecessary embarrassment.

As it turned out, this was yet another of those twists of fate that seemed to follow us around.

We just happened to be discussing what we should do next and where we should live, two fairly significant life decisions, as we strolled along the beach in Abersoch.

Logic told us that we couldn't simply buy a house. We had no income and no credit history. All we had were some savings from my Hong Kong days. So instead, we would need to buy a business that could generate an income, allowing us to build credit, with our savings used as a deposit.

The choices were limited. We knew we wanted to be in Abersoch, a very tourist driven village, so whatever we did had to sit within the tourist industry. House plus business in a tourist destination generally equals a bed and breakfast, or if you prefer, a small boutique hotel. Call it whatever makes you happy.

By process of elimination, rightly or wrongly, we decided we would buy a hotel. Grand plans indeed.

Most of the establishments in Abersoch at the time were run by older couples nearing the twilight of their careers. They tended to be old fashioned, a little dusty, and heavy on the potpourri. A couple of them were also for sale.

We approached a few local banks to see if they would help finance our new adventure, but they declined for a variety of rather ridiculous reasons. Eventually, a friend of a friend suggested we speak to someone they knew at the Bank of Ireland, who were apparently a little more flexible when it came to lending.

The fact that we could put down fifty percent in cash to match the financed fifty percent sealed the deal. Just like that, we had £120,000 burning a hole in our pockets.

Time to buy a hotel.

We viewed a few places in Abersoch but quickly found one we really liked. We put in a lowball offer which was promptly rejected. I'm not sure they took us seriously as a young couple. Well, Vanessa was young. I was youngish.

We left it with them over the weekend and thought nothing more of it.

     SIXTY NOT OUT

Time for fate and reality to collide. The reality was that the busy summer season was fast approaching. As I mentioned, the owners fell firmly into the elderly category, and the thought of another hectic season probably didn't appeal. More significantly, they had a close friend pass away over that same weekend, which seemed to focus their minds on the fact that life is precious and life is short.

They wanted out so they could enjoy their twilight years.

Which worked out rather nicely for us.

On Monday morning, we bought ourselves a hotel.

We were soon to become the proud new owners of The Wylfa Hotel.

By the time the paperwork was completed, we had around two weeks before the silly season began. That meant six weeks of back to back bookings across seven rooms, serving breakfast, evening meals, and running a bar, all handled by two completely inexperienced hoteliers, assisted by their equally inexperienced mothers.

We stumbled through it. We made a mountain of mistakes. We burnt the toast. On one occasion we even served deep fried battered mushrooms without the mushrooms. That's right. Just deep fried batter.

But we learned quickly. By the first week of September we were much wiser and had a little extra money in the bank. With the slower season approaching, we could finally start revamping the décor and modernizing the place with a more youthful touch.

It was the mid nineties, after all. Let's paint everything white. And I mean everything.

At the end of October we closed until two weeks before Easter, when the students arrived. That's a whole other story and we'll get to that. For now, we could relax and enjoy our own eight bedroom hotel with a bar, all to ourselves.

Actually, even better, let's throw a huge New Year's Eve party and charge people for the privilege. That should help cover some of the winter bills.

If our family Christmas at the hotel was anything to go by, we were in for a raucous New Year's Eve. Apart from me tripping and spilling a flaming Christmas pudding down the stairs, it all passed relatively drama free. We did, however, get plenty of practice helping ourselves to the free bar.

Well, sort of free. We had already bought all the booze, we were just drinking it now.

New Year's Eve was a different story. We were charging, and given the number of family and friends we had invited, I was confident we'd turn a decent profit.

The goal was to take enough to cover two months of mortgage payments. We managed that, with a little to spare.

Which was fortunate, because we had now booked our wedding for Valentine's Day 1996.

There seems to be a bit of a Valentine's theme developing here.

- 13 -

The Wedding

I could write and write about this forever, but I'm not going to. It's enough to say that it goes down as the single most monumental, love-filled experience of my whole life. Whatever I put on paper would come nowhere near doing it justice, so I'm not even going to try. All the feelings and emotions live on in my heart to this day. Trying to put them into words would be futile.

Here are the facts, in black and white.

As you've probably gathered by now, we don't normally do the normal thing. Why would our wedding be any different?

Both sets of our parents were divorced or separated by this stage, so for us it was an easy decision to do something a little different. And as you've seen, we liked traveling, so we decided to get married in Sri Lanka, as you do.

Cast your minds back to the days of Lunn Poly, Kuoni, and the like, when everything was chosen from a brochure. You made your selection and physically went into the shop to book your holiday, or in this case, your wedding. We were limited to certain countries because of paperwork timelines and the requirement to be in the country for a set number of days before you could legally marry.

After working through all our criteria and adding in the need for palm trees and a honeymoon in paradise, we were left with really only one choice. A Sri Lanka and Maldives wedding combo. Sounds terrible, doesn't it?

So there we were, just the two of us, off to get married.

I remember meeting a photographer and reporter from *Cosmopolitan* magazine at a hotel next to Heathrow on the morning we flew out. They'd somehow come across our engagement story and named us couple of the year, or maybe couple of the month. We were the couple of something. We got flowers, chocolate, and champagne, all of which we had to leave behind because we were flying out a few hours later. Side note, we did manage to drink the champagne. They got their story, we got to fly to Sri Lanka to get married.

We spent a fantastic week at our hotel on the south of the island, just me and my twenty-one-year-old bride. Looking back now, I realize what a huge leap of faith Vanessa made to be my partner through this life. We had navigated our issues in Hong Kong, bought a hotel, and essentially eloped to get married, and she was still only twenty-one. What a woman. Proof right there that she was my soulmate and the only person I wanted by my side as we journeyed through life.

The wedding was perfect. Just the two of us, a few elephants, some locals dressed in traditional clothing doing flips, dancing, and playing drums, and of course, one beautiful bride.

We had a full seven-course dinner, dancing, and a few drinks. Perfect.

The only small downside was that it was on my wedding day I discovered one bad oyster really could mess you up. The day after the wedding was not that pretty if you get my drift.

Luckily, that passed quickly, or passed through me quickly to be more precise, just in time for our honeymoon, which was truly spectacular. A hut on stilts over the pristine Indian Ocean on a small island in the Maldives. Quiet, peaceful, and extremely romantic.

The only hiccup there was again culinary related. I thought I was man enough to handle a hot fish curry. I was not, much to the amusement of our waiters and my new wife.

No more to add. Best wedding and honeymoon ever, which is alright with me, as I'm not planning on having another one.

- 14 -

The Wylfa

Back to wonderful, wet Wales and time to start thinking about the new holiday season. This typically ran from Easter through the last weekend in October. The summer months were filled with the usual holidaymakers. September and October brought golfers and windsurfers. Then, for two weeks prior to Easter, we were blessed with the civil engineering students from Leeds University, complete with their theodolites.

I know I sound as if I am some sort of an expert, but it's just one of those words you like when you hear it and it sort of sticks in your mind. It also seems easy to remember. Other words that spring to mind for me are epiglottis and bendigedig, which is Welsh for fantastic. That's probably my all-time favourite.

Our predecessors at the hotel had committed us to accepting these students. Hindsight would have afforded us the whits to decline. They were on a budget meal and board plan, and I mean budget. We had to provide a bed, breakfast, packed lunch, and evening meal for next to nothing. They seemed happy enough with their completely basic lunches, courtesy of Kwik Save's own-brand everything. No colour there. They did, however, make up for it with the copious amounts of alcohol they drank at night, which was definitely not discounted.

On balance, the stress on the hotel from extra people crammed into rooms and damp, wet clothing everywhere probably wasn't worth it. But the idea of at least some money coming in after the winter shutdown was hard to ignore. Amazing what you do for money.

Hotel life wasn't too bad, the fact we could take the winters off to travel was a huge plus. We escaped for long weekends to places like Prague and Granada in southern Spain. We liked the mix of destinations that had plenty of history but were also, dare I say it, trendy. Sorry, I had to use the word trendy there. I couldn't think of another one that worked as well.

Granada, in particular, had an appeal. Prague was wonderful, but I just couldn't see us living there. It did, however, teach me one thing I had been getting wrong my entire life, which is embarrassing to admit. All through my childhood, and right up until the moment I actually went to Prague, I had been singing, "Good King Wenceslaslas looked out," not "Good King Wenceslas last looked out." I genuinely thought his surname was Wenceslaslas. Standing in Wenceslas Square, I realised what an idiot I'd been. That said, I still sing the version that's forever etched into my brain.

Spain, however, was always somewhere I could imagine myself living. As far as I knew, they didn't have any kings whose names I could get wrong. I know there's a huge language barrier, but the idea of skiing in the Sierra Nevada in the morning and being on the beach in the afternoon really appealed. All of that, close enough to Granada to get a regular fix of culture and nightlife, made a very strong argument for a life in sunny Spain.

We even went back a couple of times and spoke to members of the British community living there. The conclusion was fairly unanimous. It was difficult to make money, and unless you had another way of supporting yourself, life would be a struggle. We didn't have another way of supporting ourselves. We decided we didn't want to struggle. The combination of hard work in the summer and winters off suddenly looked very appealing again.

The only place we booked and never actually went to was Amsterdam. It was my idea. The red-light district and weed cafés were probably strong contributors to the choice. They were also almost certainly the reason Vanessa wasn't too keen. In her defence, this was around the time we were considering starting a family, so we were deep into the whole "my body is a temple" phase. Amsterdam was probably the worst possible destination.

We've joked about it many times since, and I do feel a future trip is on the cards. The canals and bike rides appeal far more to me now than the red-light district or weed cafés. Who's to say we can't take a bike tour through those neighbourhoods, as long as we don't stop? I can see myself getting into all sorts of trouble in Amsterdam if left to my own devices. Best to take Vanessa with me. After reading this book, I can almost guarantee she will be.

Back at the hotel, the endless nights of standing behind the bar listening to, quite frankly, very boring people telling me their life story over a half-pint of bitter started to wear thin. Vanessa realised this way before I did and would often sneak off after dinner to read *Hello* or *OK!* Magazine in bed.

We both knew it wasn't something we wanted to do forever. It was meant to be one of our many stepping stones to better things. After a couple of full summers, we decided we'd had enough. Before the next busy season, we would put the hotel up for sale.

The trick was making our lives look idyllic. A little work in the morning, tidy the bedrooms, then off to the beach in the afternoon. We'd stopped doing evening meals by now. We had to convince potential buyers that we had the perfect work-life balance, which was very far from the truth.

They didn't need to know about the macerating toilets in four of the bedrooms that blocked like clockwork every couple of weeks, or worse, overflowed. There are only so many times you can call a plumber with the same problem before they stop answering your calls. We reached that threshold and eventually ran out of plumbers.

They also didn't need to know about the ghost that lived with us or the extreme kitchen stress over manic bank holiday weekends. Just mention eggs or lasagna to Vanessa next time you see her and watch her reaction.

A small amount of hoodwinking was required.

Before our first viewing, we ran around like headless chickens doing all the usual hotel jobs, plus a bit of extra cleaning and polishing. Five minutes before the buyers arrived, we sat down with a cup of tea, put on some gentle background music, and started reading magazines. The relaxed lifestyle vibe was alive and well, and it worked.

A lovely couple were completely convinced it was the life for them. Who were we to tell them otherwise?

The irony is that we stayed friends with the new owners and still joke about it to this day. If I remember correctly, they didn't keep it for long and adopted the same tactic when it came time for them to sell. It seems those macerating toilets worked their magic once again.

So our first home ownership experience, albeit a hotel, came to an end. It was filled with happy memories, a few not-so-happy ones, and one heartbreaking memory. A miscarriage. And it wouldn't be the last.

15

The M Word

In life, you hear the word miscarriage countless times. For most people, it barely registers. Especially as a man, it doesn't really resonate when you hear it in everyday conversation. That is, until it has a direct impact on someone you care about, or someone you love, and especially when that person is your wife.

I've always thought of myself as more of a woman's man than a man's man, if you know what I mean. Not the hunter-gatherer, alpha male type, but someone more in touch with feelings and emotions, and far more comfortable in the company of women than men. It's probably got me into trouble a few times, but I'd rather get into that kind of trouble than the kind "real men" get into. Fast cars, fast women, and fighting. Wow. Can't believe I missed out on that. In another life, maybe I will come back as an alpha male.

The closest I ever got was in my younger years, between girlfriends, when groups of us lads, including some genuine alpha males, used to hang around nightclubs waiting for what we called the ten-to-two girls. Clubs closed at 2.00am back then. I know that sounds predatory and totally unacceptable by today's standards, but when I tell you the girls openly admitted they were waiting for the ten-to-two boys to hit on them, you can see it was mutually beneficial. Anyway, that was probably as close as I ever got to being a man's man, if memory serves me right, which, as we've already established, is questionable.

Back to my more feminine self, which I'm convinced developed over time and was shaped by watching the pain my mum went through during her divorce. I sympathised with her completely and knew I never wanted to put anyone through that kind of hurt. Subconsciously, I learned to put other people's feelings ahead of my own. I knew that could make me seem wishy-washy or indecisive, but being true to my emotions and my experiences mattered more to me. If that's considered feminine, I'm happy to wear the label with pride.

So here we were, newly married and overjoyed to find out we were going to have our first child, conceived in the upper echelons of the Wylfa Hotel. By everyone's predictions, it was going to be a boy. Even the Buddhist monk at our wedding split the coconut in half and declared our first child would be a boy.

That was actually the opposite of what I had hoped. I always pictured myself as a daughter-type dad. That feminine side again. My dream was three healthy daughters, first and foremost, and if that wasn't possible, then three healthy babies, regardless.

We'll never know if the Buddhist monk was right, because at our three-month scan, no heartbeat could be found. There are moments in life that are monumental, this was one of them. I can't begin to explain the pain. You go from complete happiness and excitement at the thought of hearing your child's heartbeat to shock, sadness, and devastation in an instant.

I'm not saying it gets easier with later pregnancies, but after your first miscarriage, the joy before that first scan is replaced with worry. Constant worry. A knot of anxiety just sits in your stomach until the moment you hear that heartbeat. The innocence is gone forever. Our pregnancies would never be the same again.

You know you truly love someone when you would rather take on their pain than watch them suffer. I would have switched places with Vanessa in a heartbeat.

          SIXTY NOT OUT

I couldn't take away the emotional pain, but if I could have taken the physical pain, I would have. Watching from the outside is unbearable. Your heart is breaking for yourself, and then breaking all over again as you watch the love of your life fall apart. It is an overwhelming amount of sadness.

Healing takes time. It was winter and the hotel wasn't open, luckily. We were also in a position to escape at short notice, so we decided some time away might help. It was March, so sunshine options were limited. We were still very much in our Asia phase, so we booked an all-inclusive trip to Malaysia. Our loss coincided with a crash in the Malaysian currency, meaning we spent hundreds instead of thousands. A very small silver lining beneath very dark clouds.

What followed became a familiar pattern. As soon as the doctor gave us the all-clear to try again, we were fortunate enough to get pregnant almost immediately. Seven and a half months later, Vanessa gave birth to our first daughter, Georgiana. She arrived six weeks early and weighed just four pounds. After a week in an incubator and an overwhelming amount of parental love, she thrived and became everything we ever hoped for, and more.

Two years later, after another miscarriage in the first trimester, Olivia was born. Then, nine and a half years later, after yet another miscarriage, Tahlia arrived.

All three of them are perfect. Then, now, and forever.

It's strange how the pain of losing a baby can be softened by the joy of giving birth. It never disappears completely. I still think about the what-ifs. In my mind, the three babies we lost were all boys. Maybe we were never meant to have boys. Maybe one day that will make sense.

If there's any comfort to take from our experience, it's that our losses all happened within the first three months. I cannot comprehend the level of grief involved in losing a child later in pregnancy. That feels like a different kind of pain altogether. More painful, I imagine, than losing a parent. There is a logic to that, as painful as it is. There is no logic to burying your own child. Children should bury their parents, not the other way around. I know life isn't that simple, and it would be naive to think it is, but you can only play the hand you're dealt.

I was dealt a hand with three incredible, healthy daughters. The path to get there wasn't easy, but it was ours. And who knows, maybe my journey includes meeting the three boys we lost somewhere along the way. That would require believing in some sort of afterlife, and I'm not sure I can fully admit to that. Still, it would be nice to see those boys.

Who knows. There's still time.

Ending on a slightly lighter note, and completely unrelated to this chapter, every time Vanessa knows I'm writing my book she becomes especially kind and attentive. I'm convinced she believes I'll write even nicer things about her if she's nice to me now. Little does she know, I only ever have nice things to say about her anyway. What we've been through together is immense, and it never once crossed my mind to write about her negatively. No need to tell her that, though. I'm enjoying the extra attention and positive vibes. I reckon I can keep it going until the book's finished.

That was a heavy chapter. What do you say we dive straight into another one before returning to the day-to-day life of Abersoch?

Does anyone fancy death and divorce, or divorce and death? Grim either way. Buckle up. Here we go.

16

Death and Divorce

DD, and I'm not talking about a bra size or a pint of Double Diamond. I'm talking about Death and Divorce. Nothing can prepare you for one of these, let alone two. I know death comes to us all but divorce doesn't. Going through divorce first has a direct impact on how you view your parents' death. It sounds a bit ambiguous, but let me explain.

Eventually we are all going to die; the ultimate finishing line we cannot escape and that will come to us all. In my ideal world I will live into my 90s and when my time comes I will die in my sleep with Vanessa next to me. I acknowledge it will be a little traumatic for her, but I'm sure she will cope, and with the help of our three daughters, their husbands, and our grandchildren, she will live out the remainder of her days with a cool Italian cowboy on a farm in Tuscany. That's my dream. I'm not sure whether my parents had the same dream, or maybe a dream of their own, but if they did it sure didn't come true.

Both my parents were from West Bromwich in the Midlands...go Baggies... and both were from failed marriages before. Both never talked about their lives before they met each other, which, looking back, is really sad because I feel I only knew part of my parents: the part when they were my parents. Anything before was very gray. I remember trying to talk to them both individually about their previous lives but it was always awkward and I got the feeling they really didn't want to share. It was either from a sadness point of view or maybe there was an element of embarrassment, as I know they were married at least twice each before they got together. In fact, my dad may have been married three times before but I'm not sure. I never really had the conversation.

I wish I had, but it never seemed appropriate to ask. I have a feeling at least one of their previous partners died, which adds a whole different level of sadness in there that I wish I could have helped them work through. But they weren't the chatty type and didn't open up about their emotions easily. As a child I didn't go deep with feelings either, and I was too young to dig deep at that age anyway. It was only in later life I possibly could have addressed it, but I never got to find the right time. That's one of the negatives about traveling around the world from an early age; it's difficult to maintain a close relationship with your parents from the other side of the world.

Up to the age of eighteen I didn't have the confidence or desire to have deep conversations with my parents. After eighteen I had the added issues of not living at home anymore and my parents splitting up. Not only was it difficult to talk, but the desire wasn't there as the separation was very traumatic...well, for my mum it was. I'm not going to get into the ins and outs of what exactly happened, suffice to say my dad wasn't happy in the marriage and went elsewhere to find his happiness. I think he was rather calculating about it, and despite his subsequent protests, It's my understanding that he had already started a relationship with another lady before moving out. I mean, why would you move out unless you had sampled the forbidden fruit, right?

Anyway, it all came to a head one night as they returned from an evening out with friends. My mum came storming through the front door in floods of tears with my dad behind. My brother and I were in bed and we went down to see what was happening. Apparently, while they were trying to arrange what to do for my dad's birthday he was very noncommittal. On the journey home my mum asked him about it and he said he didn't want to plan anything with her because

SIXTY NOT OUT

he wanted to spend it with someone else. Bombshell. It transpired she was someone local and was in the friend group that all used to go out together, which made it ten times worse for my mum.

My dad moved out into his own place, apparently, and started doing his own thing. My mum just cried. As with all separations it was messy. There were times when my dad thought he had made a mistake and would try to make it work with my mum, but that just prolonged the agony for her. I remember him moving back in for a few weeks and my birthday happened to be while he was back. Round the dinner table on my birthday night he asked what my favorite present had been. I remember saying that having him back and us sitting around the dinner table as a family was the best present ever. Cheesy, but very, very true.

I don't think he shared my optimism as he moved out a few days later and they filed for divorce. My mum was broken. This is when my opinion of my dad started to change. I know it sounds like a harsh thing to write, especially after forty years, but I really, genuinely did not like my dad at this time in my life. It was twofold: not only did I not respect him as a man, I also hated him for what he had put, and would continue to put, my mum through.

I remember having the chilling realization that it would have been easier to deal with had he died, definitely easier for my mum, the grief would diminish had he died, the heartbreak of the divorce and seeing him with another woman would last a lifetime.

As you can probably imagine I was 100% team mum, my dad was not on my radar at all, in fact I don't think I had anything to do with him for about two years. My brother started to meet up with him at the pub every other week or so but I felt it was still too soon.

Eventually, with the encouragement of my mum - she had such a big heart - I started to go to the pub as well and we sort of started again, very basic and very matter of fact but it was nice to see him. I had not forgiven him but the anger had faded.

He was now living with his new wife, someone at the time I wanted nothing to do with … she was the scarlet woman, looking back now I realize it wasn't all her fault, my dad was unhappy and if it wasn't her it would have been someone else, which would have made it easier. The fact that we knew her definitely made the relationship with my dad more strained.

It made it personal.

After a couple of years together they decided to get married. Holy shit - that was one wedding I had no intention of going to. It was only after a couple of emotional phone calls from my dad's brother that I reluctantly decided to go, I stood at the back, gave my dad a hug and left as soon as I could after. I was there in person but definitely not in spirit.

After that things got a little easier with my dad and we started to hang out together more often… time definitely did its thing and the bitterness and anger went away.

Life carried on, my mum lived with Ian and I and my dad lived with his new wife.

My mum sort of made peace with herself and put all her energy into her two boys … the turning point for her was when my dad admitted to her early on after their divorce that he had probably made a mistake and he should have stayed with her, the mother of his kids, but he could not put himself through the pain and trauma coming back, maybe hollow words to make her feel better, or maybe to make himself feel better or a genuine regret we will never know but it settled my mums heart and for that small mercy I was pleased. She was still happy to get the free newspaper he dropped off most evenings on his way back to his home from his work, something we should not have condoned but it seemed somewhat satisfying to get one over on the new wife. Olive 1 - New Wife 0 … that should probably read Olive 1 - New Wife 1 as she did score my dad after all, and in all fairness I must say that in later years I really appreciated how she bonded with our girls and I truly believe she had my dads best interests at heart.

     SIXTY NOT OUT

So that's the divorce… you only get one of those with your true parents, but death, you get two.

On my mum's side there is a family history of bowel cancer, I never met my grandparents on that side, a combination of her having me later in life and them dying early. My mum's dad died in his late forties of want was then known as consumption - today we know it as bowel cancer.

She always had a dark fear that she too would die from it, she would always make throwaway comments like " well I'll never be around to see that " when we talked about our future kids growing up. I always just brushed them off and didn't worry too much about it, perhaps I should have paid more attention but at the time you never really think about one of your parents dying, it's only after and you think … could I have done anything differently?

The first warning signs were when we were away in HK in the early nineties, mum had a couple of issues with severe stomach cramps, she said she went to the doctor and he said it was irritable bowel syndrome and it would get better.

Now here lies the first question, did she even go to the doctors and secondly if she did what exactly did he say ?

I know for a fact she lived her life through my brother and I, I know for a fact that if she did have any sinister news from the doctor she would have never shared it with us. We were living our own lives, she had no one and the thought of us having to come home from HK to look after her was something she would simply not have contemplated. She would keep it to herself.

Without being cold hearted I believe her thought process would have been, I've had my life, I'm on my own,I've had my kids, they have grown up and are out in the world having fun and enjoying life. I don't want to be a burden on them, what will be will be.

Doing my math and knowing how slow bowel cancer grows, it's probable that she started with the symptoms in 1993/94 and ignored them. So all through the

Wylfa Hotel, our wedding and our first miscarriage the cancer was growing inside her. You would never have thought it from the outside, she was energetic, full of life and such a happy person. She had moved to Abersoch to be close to us and with the obvious intention of seeing out her last few years, she walked regularly, played on the bowling team - Clwb Bowlio- and even waited on in the hotel, the little posh hotel. She took great satisfaction that she could contribute and see us thriving in our new life.

One May Day bank holiday, she was not well and spent most of the time on the couch. My brother and his wife were down for the weekend so she was happy to be around us all. We had baby George and my brother had Ethan, who was about nine months old. I remember Ian and I used to be real goofy around each other and we started to sing to mum about lying on the couch. She took it in great spirits and I could tell she had a warm, smug feeling she was radiating. Seeing her two boys, their wives, and her firstborn grandchildren together, she had a look of satisfaction, like she had just finished a really heartwarming book and she had just closed it shut. Little did we know she was just finishing her own book and she knew her life was complete. She had seen everything she could have possibly hoped to see and it was her time.

The next couple of days she got progressively worse and it became apparent that she was very unwell. We took her into the hospital convinced she just had bad food poisoning or a blockage in her stomach. The word cancer was never even thought about, let alone mentioned. It was only as she settled into her bed at the hospital prior to any tests that the look in her eyes changed. She knew. She started saying that if it was cancer she didn't want to fight it; she didn't want to be a burden to anyone. It was okay if it was her time. We brushed it off like she was talking nonsense, but she knew.

X-rays came back saying there was indeed a blockage in her bowel and they would need to operate to remove it. You see, it was going to be okay. Even the doctors were calling it a blockage; there was no use of the cancer word from

SIXTY NOT OUT

them either. Still convincing ourselves everything was going to be alright, we held her hand as they prepped her for surgery and we escorted her down as far as we could go. I saw complete fear in her eyes but we reassured her it was going to be okay. We prayed and waited. But she knew.

For all the effort hospital staff put in to protect you from bad news, we got our bad news...really bad news...from a porter who was escorting us back to post-op. I asked how it had gone and he rather nonchalantly and casually said, "Yes, good, I think they managed to get all the cancer."

BOOM. I did not expect that. Honestly, I can say with hand on heart, knowing what I know about family history and mum's premonition of dying young from bowel cancer, I don't know if I had gone into protection mode but I really didn't see this coming.

Mum was in a ward one down from intensive care and didn't come around much. She had tubes everywhere and was monitored 24/7. We held her hand and brushed her hair. She came around a few times and she asked us what it was. We said they hadn't got the results back yet, which was officially correct. We thought it best not to mention what the porter had told us. As is common in UK hospitals, she contracted a bug and her temperature was spiking. Her wound got infected and she would have to go into surgery again to clean it up. This was done but now mum would be returned to intensive care.

Now I'm convinced that doctors and hospitals only drip-feed you information in small doses: a little bit of bad news sprinkled with a little hope. The avenue of hope disappears but they sprinkle a little bit more as a side order to the bad news, all the time preparing you for the inevitable. Eventually, after a couple of weeks, we had run out of good news altogether and it was all bad. But their plan had worked. We were now completely out of hope; all our possible cures had led to dead ends. They had succeeded in their quest to take all the emotions out of the picture because there was nothing more they could do. They had conditioned us to prepare for her death. Cold but true.

The only time I had any further interaction with my mum, and it was to be our final interaction, was when she came around briefly at one of our visits. She opened her eyes, looked into my soul and mouthed, "Is it cancer?" I held her hand and nodded with a tear in my eye. She sort of half-smiled, squeezed my hand and shut her eyes. She knew.

Just before she passed she was on complete life support and in an induced coma. We had gone away to get some rest for the weekend, which happened to be the Spring Bank holiday at the end of May. We had a phone call that it was probably time for us to get back to the hospital to say our goodbyes. Just over three weeks since she was first taken ill, my mum died at 12:00 p.m. on June 1st, 1999. She was 68. The machines were slowly turned off and she peacefully slipped away.

She was never a burden to anyone, least of all her children. She was an inspiration and role model who sacrificed her life so that we could live our best life.

I miss her every day.

In a perfect world I feel it would be reasonable to say that you would grieve your parents the same. But as we all know, it's not a perfect world and life's experiences shape and influence our feelings hugely. As you can see by my experiences, I was totally "Team Mum," which by its very nature means that I wasn't so much Team Dad. That was wholly a consequence of my parents' divorce and it fundamentally changed my feelings towards my father.

If you would have asked me at age twelve who my favorite parent was, or weirdly, who I would miss more when they died, I would not have been able to choose one over the other. Up until then both had done an equally good job raising me and my emotional attachment to them was equal. After my mum died, I had to reset my relationship with my dad because he was all I had left. I know her death hit him hard because it also stirred up emotions that were unique

          SIXTY NOT OUT

to him: maybe some guilt, some remorse, possibly even some responsibility? Who knows. If they were still together, she would have had something to live for, to fight for, and I would like to think he would have made her seek medical help sooner and taken on the role of carer if that's what was needed. I know that's what I would do if I was in that situation. I'm sure he asked himself those questions many times.

Over the coming months and years, he and his new wife came to visit us in Wales and I must admit we had a few fun nights. After all, he was blood and I learned to accept his choices. She took a little longer to be accepted. As I have mentioned before, she was good for my dad and she was very good with our kids; it was just difficult getting over the fact that she had, directly and indirectly, caused my mum so much pain. You never really forget that, let alone forgive. Well, I don't anyway. It wasn't helped by a comment she supposedly made with reference to my mum's age at the time of her death, something along the lines of, "Well she's sixty-eight, she's had a good life." Things like that stick in your mind and aren't easily forgotten.

I'm going to be honest, because what is the point of writing my book if I'm not going to be honest? The New Wife fell ill and also had cancer. She died aged sixty-seven. Some cold-hearted karma right there. Olive 2, New Wife 1. Full time.

Her death knocked my dad for six, for years and I mean years, he mourned her. In fact, I would go as far as to say he mourned for his life. He was morose, depressed, and very negative. I'm not judging, just calling it as it was. I cannot begin to imagine the baggage, the hurt, and the loneliness he must have been feeling; his whole world had crumbled down.

For years my dad had also been suffering from type 2 diabetes. He used to blame the jam donuts from M&S and the home brew he made under the stairs as reasons, but he managed it well and was quite fit. He played tennis to a ripe old age, which he really enjoyed. That's one good trait I picked up from him, although my serving technique is a lot less funky than his was...strange ball, hand, and arm movements that I could never replicate.

Dad's life plodded on. He lived alone, he just followed a routine, day in and day out. We moved to America, which you don't know about yet but you soon will, so the chances I had to see him were now limited. The first few years we were over there I would come back to the UK often for work, so I managed to see him five or six times a year, which was something I looked forward to. I would always stay with him the day before I flew out. We had our routine which was nice; we would go to the local pub, sit in the same seat under a display of clay pipes, and he would always order the same thing: fish and chips. I would be a little more adventurous and mix it up a little, maybe the liver and onions or maybe the chicken curry and chips. Exciting times for sure.

His health started to deteriorate slowly. His balance went and he fell a couple of times. I made a decision that I wanted to go over and see him for a few days: just some quality time with him and my brother. We visited our old village we used to live in when we were kids and bumped into a few neighbors who still lived there. It was therapeutic for all of us. Of course it goes without saying that we went to the pub, sat in the same seats under the pipes, and you guessed it, ate fish and chips.

At the time, I didn't know it would be the last time I saw him in person. It was just pre-Covid and of course we video-chatted via WhatsApp, but actually being in his presence, this was it. I guess you never know when that time is, but even if I did I don't think I would have wanted anything to be different. It truly was a special time. I think we all subconsciously knew it may be one of the last times the three of us were together. It was an unspoken cloud that was hanging over us, but it never dampened our time together and it was never spoken about.

I would have liked to have gone back one last time and it is something that I tried to do. My dad fell again and ended up in the hospital. It was during the height of Covid so travel was very difficult, but I did manage to book a flight via Paris and Amsterdam to come see him. It was cheap but very long with the layovers, not to mention all the quarantine I had to do, but it was something I wanted to do. Prior to flying out, I called the hospital to find out about visiting times and was told, in a matter-of-fact way, I would not be able to see my dad under any circumstances because of Covid restrictions, and that it was probably a waste of my time flying over. I asked how long he would be in for and they told me for the foreseeable future.

It was agreed that it was a waste of time, so I cancelled the flight. Three days later Dad was released from hospital because they needed to free up beds for Covid patients. Bloody NHS!

It turned out to be a big regret for me. I wish I had just gone, even if I had just got to wave at him through a window or something. Maybe that would have been more painful, being so close, but it was the final ten feet that I would have gone for, just to have had a hug or to hold hands one last time. To travel 4,500 miles and not be able to complete the final few feet would be some kind of cruel torture. I'm still not sure today what would have been the best decision but, at the time, I made the choice not to go and nothing is going to change that now. After all, it would have been an expensive wave.

My dad's mobility was starting to suffer now. He had long given up driving. The final straw came when he inadvertently pressed the accelerator on his car while on his driveway and careered straight into the garage, only to smash into the wall at the far end. It was probably a blessing the wall was there, as he would have ended up in the middle of his back lawn. It didn't help that the garage door was also closed, and that ended up as a mangled piece of metal on top of his prized BMW. No more driving for Dad.

My brother was very conscientious and caring, he used to regularly stop by with groceries or just to say hi. I felt so hopeless all those miles away but made sure we regularly chatted on FaceTime. The fact that I used to have complete conversations with the top of my dad's head still makes me smile to this day.

Then the call came. I knew something was wrong because my sister-in-law called. I didn't answer when I saw her name on my phone; I guess I sort of knew and needed that extra minute or so to prepare myself. I called straight back and she told me the news that my dad had died.

It transpired that he ultimately died as a result of his diabetes. He was watching TV and had a low sugar episode. He went to the kitchen to grab a bowl of ice cream and either passed out or fell and banged his head on the way down. The fact he died alone is haunting. It's such a complex issue to come to terms with, as the fact he was alone definitely contributed to his death. Had he still had a partner, they would have probably got the ice cream for him when he said he felt lightheaded and he would have carried on watching TV.

But the problem is that Dad ran out of partners. My mum had died, the new wife had died, his previous marriages had failed; it was inevitable he would end up alone. We are all going to end up alone eventually. The question is: would you rather die first, knowing that the loved ones you leave behind are all hurting, or would it be better if your partner died first and you are left mourning and caring for the family left behind, but with the knowledge that ultimately you would be left to die alone? Heavy question I know. I really don't think there is a right answer. I know I can't answer that question now; maybe down the line if circumstances surrounding health change, then the answer may become more obvious.

Over the course of our lives and over the years, there is going to be a natural change in our attitudes to life. When we are young we are carefree, fun-loving, full of energy, and excited about the challenges ahead. We are not scared of those challenges but more inspired by them; they are fuel for our adventures. As time progresses we take on more responsibility, more stress, and our ability to adapt diminishes. We become scared to take chances, nervous to take that leap of faith. What was once a challenge that excited us now cripples us with fear. What if we make the wrong choice?

Choices become monumental the older you get. As a younger version of myself, I would relish decisions I had to make. I would thrive on them. I totally embodied the gung-ho spirit. In later life those same choices are huge; the moment itself can become life-altering. What once took me seconds to decide can now take weeks, and even then I'm still not sure it's the right choice. Young person innocence is truly undervalued.

     SIXTY NOT OUT

This process is part and parcel of what we all go through. If you throw a divorce, a death, and maybe two deaths into the mix then, even with just one of these, it fundamentally changes the trajectory your life track was on. It sends you to mind-places and spaces that you never knew existed. Imagine how all three affect you. A part of your heart is ripped away and it will never be replaced. Unlike the new love we create in our hearts every time a child is born, this loss is permanent.

Your outlook on life is hardened. You become bitter for a while, you may become permanently bitter, but you definitely have a different outlook on life. Relationships matter. You also get a renewed sense of mortality, of purpose. You only get one life so you may as well make the most of it. Take some risks, have some fun, spend that money, because we are all going to end up alone and we are all going to die.

17

Footprints

Apart from making a tidy profit when we sold the Wylfa Hotel, two other things that originated there were possibly more meaningful, and they are in fact connected in a weird sort of way. Number one is Georgie, our firstborn, the second came as a consequence of Vanessa's cravings while pregnant with Georgie. Let me explain.

Just down the hill from our hotel was the beach, on that beach was Abersoch Beach Cafe, run by Derek and Elizabeth and it was home to one very tasty cheeseburger. The very same cheeseburger would satisfy Vanessa's cravings for a good few months over the summer of 1998. Being the attentive husband that I was, I would volunteer to fetch the aforementioned cheeseburger whenever the cravings happened, which turned out to be a lot. I became a regular face at the cafe, so much so that I didn't even need to order when I walked in. It was almost like bidding at an auction; a small nod of the head from the back of the queue was sufficient. I even ran a tab and settled up once a week.

On quieter days we would have nice conversations as the burger fried in the background. Elizabeth did most, if not all, the work inside, while Derek would keep an eye on things outside. This was a kooshy number, being as it was on the beach and there wasn't much to do apart from emptying the occasional overflowing bin. Elizabeth definitely got the short straw.

Now, Derek and Elizabeth were very Welsh. I don't mean that in a disrespectful way at all, in fact quite the opposite. They were extremely proud of their heritage and fought very hard to preserve it, and rightly so. Before we go any further, we have to establish the dynamics of this for those of you not familiar with the Welsh/English relationship. Imagine having an older, very annoying big brother that always thought they were right, the kind that would get all your toys out on a weekend, play with them, break them, and complain about them, then just discard them and expect you to tidy all the crap up on Sunday night. That's the English. I mean, I'm English and I saw it.

I know the roots of the issue go way back, but more recently it came to a head in the 1970s when Welsh Nationalists, aggrieved by the slow demise of their language and the influx of English buying up holiday homes, began a campaign of arson. They targeted those holiday homes as a way to discourage a further influx of English which, in turn, was a threat to their heritage, language, and cost of living. In a nutshell, the rich English moved in, drove up property prices for locals who were now priced out of the market, overcrowded all the beaches, bars, and restaurants, and clogged up the roads, all for only six months a year. They were nowhere to be seen over the winter months and yet they had the audacity to expect everyone to converse with them in English! I mean, what a ridiculous notion; people in Wales actually speaking Welsh, who would have thought it?

As with everything, there are always two sides to every equation. The obvious flip side to all this was the added value that tourism brought; locals were employed and the general standard of services was higher all year round, even when the tourists weren't there. It also meant places like Derek and Elizabeth's beach cafe were viable, and by viable, I mean profitable.

This takes me back to the conversations I used to have while waiting on the pregnancy cheeseburger, something along the lines of, if you were ever considering selling the business, then we would be interested in discussing it

          SIXTY NOT OUT

further. Now, as you know by now, I'm English. Here's me, an Englishman, asking a very proud Welsh couple to sell me their profitable Welsh business. Ballsy, right?

It was sort of a gradual war of attrition, but eventually they came around to the idea. It helped that we were already seasoned in the tourist industry (albeit only two and a half years at the Wylfa) and we were well known. Vanessa's family was well known and respected in the community, the fact that we were also going to be adding to the Welsh population definitely scored us some extra points.

It was agreed, gentlemen to gentlemen, sealed with a handshake. A mason's handshake no less, which was a complete shock to me. I remember running back up the hill and explaining to Vanessa that Derek had a huge lump on his palm and I hoped he would be okay. It's only when she explained that it was a secret Mason's handshake, and that I had failed the test miserably, that it made sense. Anyway, we were overjoyed that we would be the first person they would call if and when they decided to retire. That worked for me.

Timing was a bit up in the air. They weren't sure whether to do one or two more summers. As it turned out they did two more but, true to his word, Derek kept me in the loop, and when he finally made the decision I was the first person he called. By now we already had Georgie, had moved into a new house, and Ness was expecting baby number two, so navigating a new business was exactly what we needed. Timing was everything.

In the interim between selling the hotel and starting the new business, I had continued to model as well as renovating our new house. We bought a home at the bottom of the market and only had a minimal mortgage as we had done well with the sale of the Wylfa. Our new home needed some love, but mainly only cosmetic, so I set about doing all the menial stuff and we contracted out the other stuff to professionals.

We made a conscious decision right from our first few weeks in Abersoch to only use local Welsh craftsmen for any skilled work that needed doing. You gain respect in the community and it makes it so much easier to integrate into society.

This is something we carried through on any venture we did, either business or personal, it definitely had the desired effect. We were well accepted and, I think, even respected.

My very basic painting and handyman skills were tested to the full in our renovation and, full of glowing confidence in myself, I now turned my attention to refurbishing the beach cafe which we now officially had a seven-year lease on. The option of buying the cafe outright was discussed, but it was the world's shortest conversation. Ultimately the cafe would go back to Derek and Elizabeth's daughter, non-negotiable. After all, I was English and I don't ever think it was a consideration. I was truly blessed that they would even offer me a lease and trust me to take care of the funny little building that sat at the end of a track which led onto the beach. A funny little building that was, from that day forward, to be known as Footprints on the Beach.

The lease was signed over the winter of 2000/01, our opening day was going to be the weekend before Easter. Time to get a wriggle on. We had something along the lines of three months to totally rebrand the place, and oh, by the way, we just had baby number two. Welcome to the world, Olivia.

Sleepless nights and busy days followed, lots of busy days, but that was more my fault. As a self-confessed micromanager, I was only ever going to do all the work on the cafe myself, so no time for complaining. Let's get it done!

I completely changed the flooring, painted throughout, and installed gas griddles (a professional gas fitter did the connections before I get any backlash). I put in an extraction system, new sinks, coffee machines, instantaneous hot water, and new custom-made shelving throughout. Now, I can't take all the credit for that; a close friend, Tim, was super talented with just about everything and he made these really cool hopper things which we put crisps in. They were a kind of distressed wood and rope thing that we also used for shelves, it gave the place a cool surf-y vibe.

We worked on a menu for both drinks and food, really trying to capitalize on branding and modern twists on food. We created a whole line of custom burgers, wraps, paninis, and gourmet hot chocolates way before it all became standard fare. I guess we were trailblazers, although I hate blowing my own trumpet. But yes, we were trailblazers. I'm proud to say our Coronation chicken, big bad burger, bacon baps, and hot chocolate extravaganza are still talked about to this day!

I also paid lots, and I mean lots, of attention to our brand: Footprints. I was the first locally to import solo cups from the USA, all emblazoned with our Footprints logo. The logo was on bags, stickers, our tee shirts that the staff wore, and all our chalkboards. We did custom signs with driftwood and sand, all very creative and all designed to maximize our appeal. It seemed to work. The first year was a huge success, and the weather helped as we had one of those very rare perfect summers. We covered all areas of beach life; we sold windbreaks, dinghies, buckets, spades, kites, beach tents, everything you could imagine for a perfect day on the beach. Not to mention chocolate, crisps and ice creams. Tons and tons of ice cream.

A perfect day on the beach started with a bacon bap and coffee, followed by lunch, afternoon ice creams, and if you were still hungry at 5:00 p.m., we kicked into pizza hour and you could have pizza by the slice to go. All the time you knew that if your bucket or spade broke, Footprints was right there to sell you another one at a very exorbitant price; a much better option than having to walk back into the village for a cheaper option.

You can put all the physical things in place, but without the right energy you will never be truly successful. I felt blessed to surround myself with the most wonderful staff who completely bought into the whole Footprints vibe. Where possible I would always employ locals. I had people that would start with me in the early years and then their brother or sister would work a few years later, a few years after that another brother or sister would join the team. They were Welsh families so they tended to have lots of kids; it's so easy to find staff members when half the family has already worked for you. Between us all we created a workplace that people wanted to work in, and that shone through in buckets every time we opened the doors.

This was a magnificent opportunity to work with a multitude of local families. You know who you are, thank you. I can honestly say 95% of the guys that worked at Footprints were amazing. There were too many to shout out, some big personalities, all awesome individuals. The other 5% not so much. You probably also know who you are, so we will leave that there.

The work was hard but fun. Every season we would fall into the same routine. I did the math and I worked out we had about sixty high-season days: a week at Easter, May Day Bank holiday, Whit week, and the silly six weeks of summer. These were the days you never got back. If the rain stayed away, you would make a killing. However, if it rained on one of these days then it was a disaster, as these were the days with maximum potential. Too many rainy high-season days and your season would be disappointing, and we did have a few. As you may know, it occasionally rains in Wales.

But if it wasn't raining, then you could guarantee that the mood in Footprints would be off the scale. Music would be playing, cheeky banter with the customers, even an impromptu dance routine way before flash mobs were a thing. I sincerely think people used to come into the shop just to be entertained; we sure didn't disappoint!

Maybe a few times we went a little too far but we were oblivious to it, I think that's what made the whole thing fun: fun for us working and definitely fun for the customers. After all, let's not forget they were on holiday and their mindset was also in vacation mode, so it would have taken a lot to offend anyone.

The one thing that still makes me smile to this day is betting on the mackerel race. Every August, a mackerel race was organized by a regular. Essentially, fishermen would have a couple of hours to catch as many mackerel as possible. The one that caught the most was the winner, quite simple right? It was heavily advertised in the village and would draw crowds to watch the event. Now, I'm not

SIXTY NOT OUT

saying over the years at Footprints that we didn't have our fair share of knumpties working for us, but this took gullible to another level. By the way, that is the only word in the English language that is not in the English dictionary. Some sort of clerical error, apparently, that still hasn't been rectified. Check it out if you don't believe me.

We somehow managed to convince one of the team the race was actually a physical fish race, and the mackerel were racing from point A to point B and that they all wore little jackets with numbers on. No word of a lie. On more than one occasion we (mainly me) sent that person down to the organizers attempting to put five pounds on number three. They went, I promise you they really went. It would probably be frowned upon in today's workforce environment, but back then it was hilarious to everyone involved, including the poor gullible person attempting to put the bet on. In my defense, I let them keep the five pounds once they realized the bet was a no-go; it makes me feel a bit better now knowing I did that, but only a bit.

That prank comes close to another that we repeated on countless occasions. Not sure where this one originated from, but I have a strong suspicion that Mr. Tom Pollitt was the culprit, the little scamp. As we became busier, we found that we would be taking food orders from multiple servers, and it became confusing as the orders were written on pads with numbers between 1 and 100 at the bottom. There was also a tab at the bottom with the same number on which was returned to the customer. They would be told to listen out for their number being called once their food was ready, and the top part of the ticket would go to the kitchen for preparation.

On many occasions, we ran into a situation where the same number would appear on the pass at the same time, each relating to a different order. Many times we would hand out the wrong food to the wrong customer because they were both waiting for "number twenty," for example. What made it worse was we only had very limited seating out front, the majority of people just grabbed their food and disappeared back onto the beach. Imagine your surprise when you were

expecting a sausage roll and ended up with a Kahuna burger; a nice surprise in
this instance, assuming you like burgers that is. Compare that to the complete
opposite when you are expecting a Kahuna burger and find that you only got a
sausage roll. Not a nice surprise; in fact, very disappointing, especially if you had
walked half the length of the beach before you made the discovery.

We had to come up with a better system, we decided to add our initials to the
ticket after the number. Number 20 would now become number 20TP in Tom's
case. Foolproof, right? Yes, definitely foolproof, but also open to abuse as we were
about to find out.

Now, there is a number between 1 and 100 that can always raise a smile
or two (well, if you are of a certain age it can) and that number is 69. Now, I
can confirm we had a couple of Erin's work for us, an Emma or two, but none
of them had a last name starting with the letter R. All of a sudden, we had
a mystery employee working for us with the initials ER. You can imagine the
laughter that erupted when we started shouting out that "order number 69er"
was ready. We didn't even pronounce the E and R separately; they were merged
together and just the sound they made together was shouted. "Who's waiting
for sixtyniner?" The adults would laugh, the kids would look at their parents
wondering why they were laughing, and the parents couldn't tell them.

Very childish, but very funny. But it wasn't just a one off; it probably happened
every day over about six summers. I even tried ripping all the number 69s from
all the order pads, but somehow they would show up and off we went again. The
thing that tickled me most was the anticipation. I could see the number being
worked on and couldn't stop the childish, immature humor in me from bubbling
up. As I said before, extremely childish, but such a fond memory I cherish to this
day. How sad is that?

It was just one of the many things that kept a smile on our faces. Staff
would come and go, but the one thing that always remained the same was that
Footprints smile. That is, unless it was raining. That was the only dampener on
my mood. I think the staff were relieved, especially in the silly season as they

　　　　　SIXTY NOT OUT

would burn the candle at both ends. They worked hard and played even harder. I swear if candles had four ends they would burn all four, not to be confused with "four candles / fork handles," courtesy of the Two Ronnies!

Many times I would catch staff members sleeping off a big night in one of our inflated dinghies. These guys would be praying for rain so they could go home early. Footprints turned out to be a well-oiled machine. The location was a dream, the staff and atmosphere exceptional, and I was a good boss, if I do say so myself. I'm starting to like this blowing your own trumpet thing.

The six weeks of summer were hard, but we got into a great routine: open up, smile, have fun, serve some coffee, cold drinks, some ice cream, some food, restock, and repeat X forty-two days! We had our fair share of celebrities come into the shop also: footballers like Michael Owen and Robbie Savage, the singer Duffy, John Bishop the comedian, a snooker player called John something (sorry John something, very disrespectful I know, but fading memory and all that) and probably the most famous was Bear Grylls, of course not forgetting the odd Coronation Street actor!

By the end of August, we were exhausted but the end was in sight. The village would quiet down and we would start planning our end-of-season party! They were always very loud, very crazy, and involved huge amounts of alcohol. In the early days when I was a tad younger, I could just about keep up with them all, but as the years progressed I had to go into protective mode. After three or four beers, that was me done (I'm a well-documented lightweight). No more shots of tequila for me. Shots of water were sneakily given to me but, not wanting to lose face, I pretended they were still tequila. I pulled the funny face as I swallowed it, even over-emphasizing the strength on a few occasions by pretending to light my breath with a pretend lighter, which was in fact my thumb. You are now allowed to try that if you like. Fun, right?

We were blessed that the whole Footprints journey lasted twelve years. The initial seven-year lease was extended by three more, then right at the end, we had a couple of extra years tagged on. It was, beyond any shadow of a doubt, the best twelve-year working experience I have ever had. Everything about it was perfect. I would not change a single thing, apart from wishing it could have gone on longer, but things were changing and ultimately it would not be our decision to make anyway.

I truly believe that if I could take a snapshot of that moment, or any moment around 2005 or 2006, then that was perfection. I had my family, my Land Rover Defender, a healthy business, a magnificent home, and my health, of course. Mustn't forget that. The house was a 400-year-old cottage with a nice garden. We moved in 2005 when we were offered stupid money for our previous house; it was a huge housing market boom that, somehow, we were on the right side of. Our home went up nearly four times in value in seven years.

I distinctly remember depositing the check at our Nat West in Pwllheli the day after we closed. The cashier gave me that double-look, twice. She looked down at the check, then up at me, back down to the check, and then back up to me again. She swallowed and smiled at me. Now, I know I'm relatively attractive and used to women looking at me a certain way, but this was another level of look. It's possible she may have melted! But, as we all know by now, perfection doesn't hang around for long. In fact, we only get to recognize perfection in the past tense. It's only looking back now that I realize at that moment I had what was very close to my perfection.

I also realized that on our life journey you can really only do one thing well... well, I can, at least. We dabbled at a few things; some worked better than others. The year we opened a second location for Footprints on the road into the village didn't really excel, as we were stretched too thin.

The little clothing shop we started adjacent to the beach cafe selling beach clothes and our own merch (yes, we had our own merch before merch was a thing) that did well. It was a sister shop to Babi Bach, which we had started years before selling kids' clothes. Initially, that was a way to dress our kids in cool clothes without having to spend a fortune, but the store did well, driven by Vanessa and her amazing buying and merchandising skills which are still evident

     SIXTY NOT OUT

to this day. It did so well that we also had a second Babi Bach store in Pwllheli. That led us to opening another boutique in Abersoch called Seren. This didn't do too well! You see the pattern here. All along, in the background, Footprints was ticking over, year after year doing its thing. In retrospect we should have just stuck with that, with a light sprinkling of Babi Bach.

Back to our idyllic life in our old cottage: I loved it here because I could potter. Men like to potter; it keeps them out of mischief. I would work incredibly hard, every day, for about nine weeks a year. The rest of the time Footprints was open I would still work, but it was more relaxed. Come Halloween, we would close the shop down for the winter and I would have time to potter. I might be in my shed, I might be cutting my grass, I might be having a bonfire, but whatever it was, I was pottering. I miss pottering.

I would always have a winter project. My favorite of which was building a patio area made from Welsh slate. It took me all winter, but it was worth it. I can't take all the credit, however; some of the skilled wall building was done by a friend, Geraint, and also a father-and-son team that rebuilt most of our walls around the whole property. They were very traditional and the finished job was perfect.

We had used them when we renovated the shop in Pwllheli. I did the manual stuff, like individually scrubbing each stone we had uncovered after removing plaster from the walls. It took about six solid days to expose them all, including the old wooden beams. Bloody hard work, but by heck it looked good when we varnished them. John and his son were invaluable as they were experienced working in Welsh stone, which made them perfect for my wall restoration at home. And they were local. Always use the locals, just like the local electricians I used to rewire my swimming pool. Oh shit, forgot to mention we had a swimming pool. Told you Footprints was good. It gets lots of use in Wales, does that swimming pool, Gulf Stream or no Gulf Stream. We had palm trees in our garden, don't you know!

So, when I wasn't pottering, we were fortunate enough to have the option to travel over the winter. Sometimes with the kids, sometimes without. We had a built-in babysitter in Vanessa's mum, that made it easy. Trips with the kids were fun; we would regularly go to see Vanessa's dad in Menorca, because that's where he lived, or Cyprus to see Vanessa's mum, because that's where she lived part of the year. I just had a dad that lived in Wheaton Aston; that's what I brought to the party!

But the trips I took with Ness were different, if you know what I mean. Just a few days away: maybe Prague, Granada, or Florence. All rather sophisticated, don't you think?

Florence was actually our first trip to Italy together, made that much more special because we went to celebrate our tenth wedding anniversary. Just being able to wander around the city on foot was perfect. We could stop for coffee in the morning wherever we liked and in the evening for wine. On a few occasions we actually stopped for wine in the morning, which was always followed by coffee super early the next morning. Hangovers in Italy; is there any better place to get over a hangover? All the art, culture, and architecture was just up our street. Literally, it was just up the street from our hotel, a stone's throw from Ponte Vecchio. That's if you could throw a stone a long way, of course.

Ness was still in the early stages of perfecting her technique to always get us a room upgrade. She is a seasoned professional now, but back then it still took a little friendly persuasion. As is my thing, I book the initial room: comfortable, practical, and affordable, though not necessarily in that order. You'd think I would have learned my lesson by now. If it's just me or a quick overnight stop somewhere on a road trip, then my choices are usually acceptable, most of the time anyway. Ask the girls about Macon, Georgia when you see them.

I realize for my tenth wedding anniversary I probably didn't go the extra mile that I should have. I got the right hotel in the right area, just not the classic Italian suite with floor-to-ceiling mirrors, wooden floors, original artwork, and a four-poster bed. Vanessa managed to get that room, however, with little to no effort.

     SIXTY NOT OUT

It's now a standard family joke that we don't unpack until after Vanessa has been down to see the manager and secured the upgrade. I kid you not, 90% of the time she is successful. The other 10%, we leave!

It was actually on one of our trips to Andalusia that we started talking for the first time about the possibility of living abroad permanently. Not surprisingly it came at the end of a drink-filled evening, but it was a real conversation and real things were discussed. It was something we would start talking seriously about over the next few months.

As you can imagine, living in a four-hundred-year-old house has its challenges, not least the roof. Obviously, it's not that old, unlike the walls, but the flat roof at the back, a mere spring chicken at twenty-five years old, was starting to age. To compound matters, the rear of the house was built on solid rock. Apparently, dynamite was used to create enough of a hole to build the extension; in my opinion, not enough dynamite was used. Any rain we had would cascade down the rock, Victoria Falls style, straight into the wall. I would even hazard an educated guess that some of that rainwater seeped into the house under the floor. The mushrooms growing on the bedroom carpet in the winter were the giveaway.

A little friendly advice to any potential home buyers out there: if possible, try to buy your house at the worst time of the year, with the worst weather possible. In our case, that's winter. Every leak, damp spot, or funky smell will be very evident. Buy in the summer and it's much easier to miss these things, or much easier to disguise them. No wonder most houses sell in the spring or summertime; they smell better!

We've established we had a damp problem, the decking at the back was also rotten, and the flat roof was patchy. Not enough, on its own, to make you consider selling after only three years, but you have to factor in the damp weather and our crazy nomadic lifestyle that always bubbled just under the surface. Factor in more and more trips away to fabulous warm places, and the calling to move on kept getting stronger and stronger.

We had discussed moving to Australia. We both loved it, the people, the lifestyle, and the weather, but the only thing that stopped us investigating it further was the distance. It was just way too far away from everyone. Ultimately, it was the distance that made Australia a no-go. We had been to Andalusia a few times and particularly liked the Costa Tropical area around La Herradura. It was close enough to Granada for that cultural city fix, but also in the foothills of the Sierra Nevada to get a winter mountain fix. Plus, it was only a two-hour flight from the UK. It ticked many boxes.

My box was definitely ticked, but it was Spanish speaking, obviously. Going from a tight-knit Welsh-speaking community into a tight-knit Spanish-speaking community was a little daunting, after talking to locals we discovered it was difficult to make any money there. We put it on hold for a while, but one thing we had established was that we wanted warm weather, somewhere relatively close, and preferably English speaking.

There was no rush to decide, because we had arranged a family trip of a lifetime: we were off to see Vanessa's best friend and her family in the USA. It was a place I had never really thought of going. I didn't like the thought of America, but two weeks in the Florida sun in October seemed very appealing. Accommodation was free, flights were cheap, and the dollar-to-pound ratio was almost two-to-one. I mean, Florida wasn't too far away, the weather was nice, and they spoke a sort of English.

Oh, no. It couldn't. Could it?

Decision USA

It all started off so innocently. It was a family holiday visiting our friends in Florida: nice food, wine, warm weather, warm blue sea, big fluffy beds, and houses with swimming pools. I guess we were used to that, but these were houses with pools that you could use twelve months a year. And it was cheap; boy, was it cheap. Even factoring in a favorable exchange rate, it was still cheap.

Trouble is, that's when your mind starts racing. All the "what ifs" come out to play. What if we sold our house and bought a dream home overlooking the water with sunsets to die for? What if we bought a fancy convertible Jeep and cruised up and down Clearwater Beach? What if we bought a small boat just to potter around in? After all, we know I like to potter.

Trouble is, all these what ifs were possible. I think that's where the problem started. I mean, someone should have pinched us right there and then. We were dreaming. We were on vacation, damn it! We mustn't forget we are on vacation. We were on holiday; it was still a holiday at that stage, not a vacation. You see where I'm going here. Holidays and real life are two separate things. The edges blur sometimes, but it's very difficult to replicate that holiday mode into real life.

I don't think it helped us that our hosts showed us a really special time. They took us to all the best restaurants, introduced us to some nice people, and helped us avoid some of Florida's uglier sides. I remember coming from the airport we had to come a specific scenic way so as to avoid the monstrous-looking eight-lane road otherwise known as US 19. The extremely ugly road that is US 19.

By the end of our two weeks, we were starting to get that Florida vibe. We were made to feel very comfortable, very accepted, and the fact that Suzy and Vanessa had known each other since school...yes, the same Suzy as before, small world...definitely added to the relaxed vibe and the pull that Florida was starting to have over us. There was plenty to think about on the plane home and over the coming months.

I'm not sure how much time we gave it or how much research we did, but whatever it was, it wasn't enough. The trouble with nomads, and gung-ho nomads at that, is they make a decision pretty quickly and then find facts and scenarios that will support that decision, instead of looking at facts and scenarios first and then making a decision based on that. I guess we are just wired differently; it has its advantages and disadvantages.

We made the decision to move to Florida pretty quickly and we would fill in the blanks later. After all, if we made a mistake we could always come back, couldn't we? Trouble is, you can't just sell up and move to Florida. There are ridiculous hoops to jump through first. The first decision was which visa we would apply for. It was confusing, as the only visa I knew about was my Barclaycard and its ever-growing balance!

It was a case of eliminating which visas we weren't eligible for and seeing what was left. Any skilled visa was thrown out. Any company-sponsored visa was not an option. We were down to investment visas. There were varying degrees of investment, including one where you basically buy a qualifying US business which employs a certain number of US workers. As long as you stick to the criteria and remain in business, then you are okay. If the business fails, then you have to leave the country. That was too much uncertainty for a man with a family.

　　　　SIXTY NOT OUT

We needed to go for something that gave us security, a way to a green card and ultimately the road to citizenship, if that's what we wanted. We wanted one that would let us live and work anywhere in the US. Go big or go home, right? We probably should have gone home, but that's only a comment in retrospect, we decided to explore going big. That meant the EB-5, the all-singing, all-dancing visa. Some would call it buying a green card; I would call it selling everything you ever owned, everything you ever worked for, and rolling the dice on a life in America. It required a $500,000 investment in a business in a targeted employment area that created ten US jobs. That was the easy part. The hard part was picking the right one.

There were numerous choices. We whittled it down to a few options. We knew we wanted something that was backed with real estate. We wanted a clear exit strategy and, although the investment had to be deemed "at risk" to qualify for the visa, we wanted one with a clear path to repayment, which was also highlighted in all the prospectuses we looked at. Put all this in the mixer and what do you get? You get Jay Peak Ski Resort, Waterpark, and Hotel in Vermont: the poster child of the EB-5 program, backed and audited by the State of Vermont. This was it. We would do some more research and more due diligence, but we felt we had made our decision. Let's get the ball rolling.

Just Vanessa and I flew out to Florida for a quick trip to meet up with our immigration attorney. He was obviously very lawyerish, very careful not to say anything that could come back and haunt him (or come back and sue him), but the gist of what we got was that Jay Peak appeared to be a good choice. If we were willing to take the gamble, then Jay Peak would be in the top three of his selections. See what I mean about playing it safe? It was sort of reassuring to us.

Back in the UK, we were now living in limbo, or to put it another way, we were living in rented accommodation. Little did we know but this would be something we would get very familiar with. This is coming from the man currently living in his 17th (seventeenth) rental. Glad I could get the parentheses in there, similar to when a football score gets above a certain number and the BBC uses them to avoid any confusion!

There we were with an extraordinary amount of money in the bank, just waiting to make that investment. Timing wasn't perfect; we had just missed Phase One of the Jay Peak offering, we decided to wait for Phase Two to become active, which was apparently a few months out. We had been told all along that when you are in the application process for a visa, it is unwise to visit the US. We knew the whole application thing would take about ten months, so we decided to get a quick trip back in to see Florida one more time. It was a little two-week getaway before all the boring, tedious paperwork started. What a carefree life we lived!

This didn't turn out to be everything we expected. Unbeknownst to the kids, Vanessa was actually in the early weeks of pregnancy, we knew we wanted a more relaxed and chilled vacation, which we got. We had discussed for years the possibility of having baby number three. Now, I'm not going to lie, I was more skeptical. We had two, got them out of nappies, into school and life was good. Life seemed easy. Maybe too easy? We even had Cookie, our Cocker Spaniel. Why rock the boat? Actually, why not rock the boat? I've always said that Vanessa's desire to have another child was greater than my desire not to have one. We rocked the boat!

Unfortunately, you cannot reason with Mother Nature, and towards the end of the holiday we started getting signs that all was not well with the baby. The last few days were hard as reality was setting in and the signs were not good. It was also something we chose not to share with the girls at that time, balancing their happy times with our secretive sad times was tough. I think we were both relieved just to get back to Wales, but there was no hiding the fact Vanessa was having miscarriage number three.

The pain is still the same, the hurting the same, and the helplessness is the same. But somehow, seeing my dear wife go through this for a third time, it seemed a lot worse. Why us? Looking back now, we rationalize and are grateful that we were blessed to have children ultimately. Many couples go through the pain time and time again with no hope of ever achieving parenthood, so I realize the blessings. We hold onto the dream that the three babies we lost are our three boys and they are somewhere looking down on us, guiding us and helping our daughters navigate this world down here on Earth. They seem to be doing a good job thus far!

If we stick to following the original formula, what comes next? Yep, another pregnancy. But this time, it would affect our plans to go to the US. It's funny how things have a way of falling into place. Vanessa fell pregnant again immediately. I put that down to her super-fertile side of the family and, as much as I would like to take some sort of credit, I really don't have a strong argument to suggest otherwise.

Her first trimester, the scary one for us, coincided with the final three months we had to wait before we could submit our application to Jay Peak. Once we were out of the woods with regard to the pregnancy, we were in a position to file our application with Jay Peak, which is a mountain ski resort in Vermont with lots and lots of woods. Time would tell, but we were far from out of the woods with Jay Peak.

The initial application was straightforward. We registered our interest in Phase Two, received an offering package and prospectus to go through, and spent a little time reading it all. It was filled with overtly positive sales leaflets, glossy brochures, and endorsements from leading Vermont politicians backing the project. They doubled down on the fact that this was the only project to be backed by and audited by the State of Vermont. There were even links to videos of Vermont Senators talking about how good this opportunity was. I mean, that was the cherry on top of the already very appealing pie.

Once accepted into the project, it would lead to a provisional two-year green card for me, followed by the conditions being lifted, then, after five years, the option to pursue citizenship. The beauty was that I could bring my wife and any children under twenty-one along as well, they would also be able to follow the green card path. It was a nice, tidy package on paper.

It all made sense, the decision to go with Jay Peak was less of a decision and more of a natural progression. It was head and shoulders above all the other options. It was almost like it was too good to be true. A huge red flag missed there! I cannot emphasize enough that at that moment I was 100% sure this was the right path for us to take. I had spoken to numerous people. Some were connected to Jay Peak, who I know probably had a vested interest in keeping me sweet, but there were also people with no connection or anything to gain from me signing up. Everyone seemed to think it was a no-brainer. Jay Peak was promoted as the poster child of the EB-5 visa program and I agreed with them. Well, I know I did, because the next week I was inquiring how and where to send my deposit.

The ball was rolling with regard to Jay Peak. This was something that would take on a life of its own. The whole application process, which also incorporated applications to the US immigration service, was like a snowball rolling down a hill. There was an extraordinary amount of paperwork that had to be completed as part of our package. We needed a paper trail of every dollar we were investing. It was thorough, but it was nothing we didn't have; it was just extremely time-consuming. Now, all of this was being done under my name. I was the individual investing in Jay Peak and, if everything worked out, I would have the ability to bring my family along for the ride, however big that family was.

The other side of the coin was coordinating with the US Embassy in London for our interviews once approval from Jay Peak and USCIS was granted. This was for the whole family, and we technically had four-and-a-half people at that stage; Tahlia was still in the oven. It was stressed to us numerous times that our best plan was to have Tali in the UK before emigrating. It would keep the paperwork easier and be a lot cheaper. It created a small delay, but nothing that couldn't be overcome.

Here we were, onto our second rental in Abersoch. Our first year of renting in Mynytho had come to an end and it was mutually agreed that we wouldn't stay on for a second year. This was a combination of a damp house, a crazy landlady, and another baby on the way. I will say the view was very nice and the back garden was big, but that's as far as the positives go. I'm sure they have fond memories of us also.

The Abersoch rental worked so much better. We were closer to everything and we had a little more space, which was perfect. On February 6, 2010...which in British speak is 6/2/10...at 10:26 p.m., weighing 6lb 2oz, baby Tahlia was born. Our family was complete! We also now knew how many applications we had to complete for our visas, including their names and dates of birth. Our US Embassy ball was now rolling as well.

I'm not sure if we really had any doubts about what we were doing. We were just putting one foot in front of the other and it was slowly leading us to a new life in America. If we did have any reservations, then now would have been the time to express them. But Vanessa was too busy with Tali and I was just plodding through the mundane paperwork and preparing for another Footprints season. We were completely oblivious but the chance to question our decision was slipping by. We were too busy, and perhaps too naive, to take a step back and take one last look at whether it was a sensible idea or not. In reality, we were far too invested to back out now. We had sold our house and, instead of looking back, we were committed to finding a better life for our family. That better life, we thought, was in the USA.

Up until now, we had only committed a deposit to Jay Peak: something along the lines of $15,000 so they could begin the paperwork. But the time was nearly here to throw in the whole kitchen sink. The balance was something along the lines of about $535,000. It pains me to write that so I sort of pretend it was about that much, in a flippant way. But deep down, I know the whole investment thing cost us exactly *$550,000*. That number is ingrained on my hear. Well, the time was here to pay up, and pay up we did. No going back now. It was just a waiting game. All the paperwork was in, we just had to wait for our embassy appointment to come through.

Tali was growing, Footprints was ticking over nicely, and the two older girls were finishing out their school years. We finally got notification of our appointment and, after we gathered all our embassy documents and medical records, we headed down to London. I remember it being a straightforward sort of day: lots of security, long lines, and a bizarre secondary medical check where we had to, among other things, prove that we were the sex we said we were. It was in fact established at that time that I did indeed have a penis and therefore I was a man! Good to know.

We eventually got our time in front of the interviewer. I remember being extremely polite and courteous, as if that would guarantee me entry into the US. I think that and the fact all our background checks were clean all but sold the deal. We knew everything was going to be smooth sailing because on our way in we ran into Robbie Williams. We had convinced ourselves that he was our lucky charm. We even exchanged a few words, but don't tell anyone. It wasn't as many as I exchanged with Ant and Dec in The Blue Elephant Thai restaurant, but that's because I'd had a few beers and the Dutch courage had kicked in.

Anyway, we were approved and our passports had their visas applied before we left. It was all coming together.

By this stage we had moved into temporary rental number three: a fully furnished flat owned by one of Vanessa's friends. It was a full-circle moment as it was right opposite The Wylfa. We were basically living out of suitcases by now, as all our bigger belongings were on a ship on their way to temporary rental number four in Florida. We had to strategically plan every aspect of the move with total precision. The boxes which contained all that was left of our worldly possessions were due to arrive and be transported to our Florida address sometime around September 15, give or take a day or two. We knew we had to fly out the week before, which coincidentally was at the end of the Footprints "silly season." Now, if you throw Cookie the Cocker Spaniel into the mix, you have all the elements that had to be synchronized.

September 9 was the day. The flight out of Gatwick was relatively early, so we decided to travel down the day before and stay in a hotel close to the airport. I don't think the goodbyes were a big thing as most of the close family had already booked flights to come out to see us as soon as we had settled, and I was flying back to close up Footprints at the end of October anyway, so no big fuss was made.

The night in the hotel was horrendous. There were five of us and a dog in a cage in a room designed for three if you were privileged. The only upside was that I didn't have to wake up early to take Cookie to the cargo side of the airport, not because her check-in time was late, but because I didn't get any sleep anyway. There was no waking up to do. I remember she had to be checked in four hours before the flight. Her papers were checked and she was good to go. See you on the other side of the pond, Cookster! I returned to the hotel, woke everyone up as they had fallen back to sleep, and bundled them into the car for the short ride to the airport.

I remember feeling excited that all the planning had been done and all the hard work of the applications was complete. We could now start our new life. I feel like the girls were a mix of excitement, apprehension, and sadness. We were taking them away from everything they had known and everyone they had known; how could they not feel nervous and scared? But it was a gamble we were taking. Hopefully it would work out. I know now about their reservations, so that's probably not my story to tell. Maybe one day they will write their own recollections and contradict my perspective. Well, the older two might. I don't think Tali will be writing her thoughts of that time as she was only seven months old and was happy to go with the flow.

The flight was non-eventful. We arrived on time in Orlando and, after spending a little extra time going through immigration as our papers had to be double-checked on our first entry point, we picked up the rental car, loaded up the bags, and headed to the other side of the airport to be reunited with Cookie.

I swear that from about two minutes out, we could hear her. She was crying, yelping, and woofing as only dogs do. I forgot to mention she was such a dependent dog. All the time Vanessa was nursing Tali, Cookie had taken it on herself to reinvent herself into my baby, and I fell for it hook, line, and sinker. She even slept at the bottom of our bed every night. If it got cold she would also get under the blankets with us, but don't tell anyone that as I know it's frowned upon.

From a long way off we could hear baby Cookie crying, from the moment we entered the cargo area and she heard our voices, the decibel level went up another notch. They were glad to get rid of her. Bless her, she had been cooped up in a cage for over twelve hours with only water to drink. She was beside herself, so much so that she had pissed all over the cage at some stage and managed to rub herself in it. She was soaking wet and she smelt something rotten.

She was so happy to see us and was trying to jump up at us, but she smelled terrifically bad that we found it hard to love her back. Quickly we found a small hose somewhere and managed to dilute the piss smell a little, enough to give her a proper welcome anyway. After throwing all her soiled bedding away and...because it was too big...the travel cage we spent £100 on, we managed to coax her back into the car. I think a lot of bribery with treats was called for, but eventually we got her in.

We added her to the already overflowing car. Vanessa drew the short straw and carried her on her lap. We pointed the car south and headed to our new life in Tampa Bay. We were one Motley Crue: mum and dad unsure if they had made the right choice, two older daughters convinced that their parents had *not* made the right choice, one seven-month-old baby screaming for milk and finding it hard to adapt to the stifling humidity, and one yelping dog that still smelt of piss.

Oh, joy! Welcome to the U.S.A., Woodings. Have a great day and don't forget to drive on the right.

     SIXTY NOT OUT

19

The Dream/Nightmare Begins

Home number one was always going to be temporary. It was a cute, typical American style. Nothing fancy, but everything seemed big: big kitchen, big TV, big beds, and a big garage. That garage was important, as all our worldly belongings were due to be delivered the following week. House one was our staging post, a base camp where we could get our bearings, adapt to a completely different lifestyle, and begin all the mundane tasks of getting phones, registering the dog, getting social security numbers, and enrolling the kids in school. We had only rented it for six weeks, so we also had to find somewhere to move to within that timeframe. Much to Vanessa's displeasure, I also had to go back to Footprints to close up for the season towards the end of October.

This was the start of a two-year crazy commute. It turned out to be a blessing, as we were guaranteed two years more money from our Welsh money-making machine. I would have to fly back six times a year but, at the time, flights were cheap and we still had to make sure we nurtured the goose with the golden egg. It also turned out to be a curse, having that regular money from Wales come in. We relied too heavily on it and didn't really look into money-making ideas in the US. Our Welsh money, combined with our savings and the promised quarterly payments from Jay Peak, meant life was cozy. Or, at least, it appeared that way.

The boxes we shipped from Wales three months earlier arrived. We counted 108 when we loaded them and I counted 108 when we unloaded them. It is a strange conundrum I will never understand. We received everything we shipped, yet over the next few years, we realized we were missing a few things that were definitely in those boxes. But they are gone. Namely, a nice corduroy jacket I had…and stop laughing. I still have visions of a deckhand on one of those cargo ships parading up and down in said corduroy jacket. Despite all the giggles, I bet he looks good in it!

We adapted to life relatively quickly. The dollar-to-pound exchange was still strong and life seemed cheaper in Florida. Our rental car was big and chunky compared to what we were used to, and the process of getting our US driving license was as simple as reversing into a parking space in a parking lot. It's a good job everything is bigger over here, including the parking spaces. I know that even Vanessa wasn't phased by that maneuver. It was "Easy Peasy," which is something that cannot be said about the girls' first day of school.

Imagine two young girls who grew up in a very quiet, safe, secluded village in Wales. Their primary school had just twenty students and everyone knew each other. Imagine the torment they must have been feeling when they realized they were just about to enroll in schools that had hundreds and hundreds of kids. As parents, we were naive and hadn't thought this through, but our kids certainly had.

On the first day they were going into school, Liv actually crawled under the bed and refused to come out. Such was her anxiety. I truly believe we had to physically pull her out, and she was gripping the carpet similar to how a cat would if it didn't want to be picked up. It was very traumatic, mainly for her, but also for us as parents. The magnitude of our choice to come to the US was starting to kick in. Georgie, being of a different character, was also traumatized but she kept hers inside and stayed quiet. We tried to convince ourselves that she was okay, but the reality was they were both very nervous about those first few days and weeks in school. And rightly so. It was a huge emotional rollercoaster we forced them on and probably something that has scarred them for life, or at

        SIXTY NOT OUT

the very least affected their early development years. Sorry, girls, for putting you through that. Don't hold it against us.

I think, with time, they settled in but it was hard for them initially. They were the new kids with strange accents and, as we all know, kids can be cruel.

We made a few friends, although they were mainly friends of Suzy and Dillon. That led us to the opportunity to take on a lease for a home in Palm Harbor; Cobb's Landing to be exact, affectionately known as "Snobbs Landing." Our first permanent address in Florida was to be on Fox Squirrel Drive and our landlord was Mr. Farid.

Don't get me wrong, it was a lovely home. It was a little bigger than we probably needed and was in need of a little love, but it was perfect for our family. It was also a perfect home for welcoming our guests and family from home. We knew they were chomping at the bit to come see us, and come they did. My dad came, my brother and his family came, Vanessa's dad came, her sister came, and her mum came. And you know what? Jenny, Vanessa's mum, was the only one that ever returned. We don't take it personally, honest, as I know we are fabulous hosts, but we just assumed over the years that maybe Florida wasn't their thing. I get that now. We can give a pass to both our dads who didn't return more for health reasons, but I truly thought the rest of the family would come out more.

Again, looking for a positive out of a negative, it made the core five of our family so close. It created a sort of "us against the world" mentality which is still evident today. Tali didn't know too much about it at the time, being only seven months old, but she gets it now!

A definite upside of renting is that if the house has any issues, then it's on the landlord to get it fixed. We worked through a few of those at Fox Squirrel. But as our one-year lease was coming to an end and we were given the option to buy, all of a sudden a house that we knew inside out, with all its flaws and all the flaws we had fixed, became a very appealing proposition. We were also coming from a place with limited options. We hadn't built any credit as we couldn't get a credit card since we were not working in the US. We were just living off the Footprints wages, therefore we were not eligible for a mortgage.

Luckily for us, we were on a strong, positive run at this stage. In fact, life was good and rosy. Farid said he would finance the house as long as we could come up with a 10% deposit. We had already bought a couple of nice cars for cash... well, one nice one and a Volvo, the "Volverena" as it would affectionately be called...but we still had enough left to come up with the deposit. So that was it, simple as pie. We bought a house in *Snobbs Landing*, albeit at the cheap end of the prestigious community.

This is where we thought we would fit in. This is where we thought we belonged. We aimed too high. This was to be the start of our downfall. Years and years of hard work, good fortune, and a high quality of life had just peaked. We didn't know it yet, but from this moment on, things changed. And not for the better.

At the time the shift wasn't noticeable. But looking back now, it is as clear as day that this was our high point in Florida. From that point on, it feels like the world turned against us, kicked us, and spat us out. The real scary thing is that this was thirteen years ago and we have been through shit for thirteen years. Unlucky for us! There were some high points, as you will see, but for the most part, it has been soul-destroying. Hang on tight, it's about to get very dark.

Now, Cobb's Landing is a very upmarket neighborhood, a collection of high-end homes on the shore of Lake Tarpon. It is quintessentially American: quiet during the week and home to family get-togethers on weekends. The reason it was quiet in the week was because all the owners were out working hard to pay for their homes in Cobb's Landing. That was a small detail we overlooked.

I remember talking to some of the neighbors, at least the ones that weren't medicated or bat-shit crazy, and they said they often wondered what I did for a living because all they ever saw was me mooching around in the yard or walking Cookie. I guess that should have set the alarm bells ringing, but I was happy in my bubble. I was commuting back to Wales to oversee the last year of Footprints, had two cars paid for, some savings, and the potential to get a quarterly check from Jay Peak. "Smug" is a word that pops to mind.

As Footprints came to an end in October 2012, I really didn't have a plan in place. I unknowingly fell into my age-old routine of taking the winter off, something I had done for the last twelve years. I don't mean I sat in a chair for five months, but I took a step back and went into semi-hibernation. I didn't acknowledge the fact that there was no Footprints income coming in March, which meant no more money. We had a financial cushion, but the reality is that the cushion is there for a reason: to protect against unforeseen expenses. It is not to be used to live on, because then you no longer have a cushion; you have a situation. After thirteen or fourteen months in the house, we had a situation.

Now, I'm not a lazy person by any stretch of the imagination, but we were in a predicament where I really needed a job. All I had ever done was work for myself. I had no degree, which is frowned upon in the US, and no skill set that would make me attractive to potential employers. Plus, and it's a big plus, we hadn't come to Florida to work for someone else. We had to find something we could do ourselves. We took the wise words of Farid to heart when he said we should create something around who we are as individuals, something that makes us unique and stands above all the noise. People always invest in people, not ideas. We had to think of something.

Admittedly, I did a little modeling through some agents in Tampa, but it was a big change from the days of London and Barcelona. There were no more nights driving up and down the Ramblas in the back of a convertible eating boxes and boxes of Twix. One bite, smile, throw it on the floor, open another one, and repeat, repeat, repeat. I started at least thirty-five Twix that night. I never finished one. I still haven't finished one to this day! It's a bit like the whisky scenario but with chocolate.

My best Barcelona job by far was for Coke. It was obviously in Spanish and they were going to dub an authentic Spanish speaker over the top of my voice.

But I had to say the words in Spanish so they could match up my lips with the voiceover. As a non-Spanish speaker, it is a lot harder than you think, but I pulled it off. I still know the words to this day. The English translation is: "Whatever food you are eating, it tastes better with Coca-Cola." I am now saying that in Spanish to myself and if you would like me to say it out loud, then please just find me and ask. I digress, for a change.

I managed a few modeling jobs in Tampa. I felt by now I had grown into my face. By that I mean I always felt like a wrinkly young person and now I felt more like a wrinkly older person with more defined features. I was comfortable in my skin, which for much of my life I was not. Whether it was the freckles and skinny frame from my school years or my puffy, tired-looking face in my early years of modeling, I was now older and more rugged, and I was good with that.

What I shouldn't have been good with was the lack of money coming in. If you throw in a little maintenance here and there, a couple of small improvements, a property tax bill, a house insurance payment, and a mortgage, then that cushion starts to deflate pretty rapidly. On the horizon, we had an AC that was about to pack in and a roof that would need replacing in a year or so. These were big expenses with not enough money coming in to cover them. The alarm bells started ringing. They are still ringing!

Call us foolhardy for not having a plan in place, and I accept that, but we have always been "fly by the seat of your pants" type of people. It had worked so far so we were always optimistic. We may have to use unconventional methods sometimes, but we always stumbled through. We always made our payments. "Fake it until you make it," right? We always thought we would make it.

We were promised quarterly checks from Jay Peak of about $10,000. That's what we expected. That's not what we got. We were thankful to get $4,000 or $5,000 on a couple of occasions, and that was when two quarters had been rolled into one. They blamed small operational issues which would be fixed once the phase we had invested in was complete and started to create a revenue stream.

 SIXTY NOT OUT

"Hold tight, it's coming," that's what they said and we believed them. Why wouldn't we?

We thought about going to the bank to re-mortgage, but we had no credible US income so we would not have qualified. With that being said, we approached some friends, who shall remain nameless, to see if we could work out some sort of short-term loan, just until we could get our next project up and running. I mean, you know you are in financial trouble when your wife rings you up and asks which credit card to put the two coffees on that she is just buying at Starbucks. I know it's expensive there, but come on!

Until you've actually had to do it yourself, you don't realize how humiliating, embarrassing, and nerve-wracking it is to go to someone you know very well, cap in hand, and explain to them your position. You have to explain that you need help, not just financially but mentally also. It's about as big as it gets, especially coming from a supposed place of security and comfort. We had never imagined in our wildest dreams that the shit would hit the fan so quickly.

We asked, explained our situation, and were open to any help they were willing to offer. Unfortunately, none was forthcoming. I understand why, but at the time it got very tense. Words were exchanged and friendships were put on rocky ground. I admit you have to look at it from both sides. Here we were, in trouble and highly emotional, asking for help. We didn't want a handout, just a helping financial hand to help guide us through troubled waters. We offered guarantees as much as we could and it was always going to be something we returned, with interest, over time.

We were hopeful that something could be arranged as we knew they had the financial means to help. I guess we just saw it as a case of: if they wanted to help, then they would. I think the fact that it was dismissed outright and with no real sympathy was upsetting to us both. I know we didn't have any right to expect any help and we might sound misguided to even think it was an option. Hell, you might even think that we are at fault for putting them in that position.

But one thing both Vanessa and I know for sure, with 100% certainty, is that if the roles were reversed and we were in a position to help a friend who genuinely needed help, then we would help. What's the point of financial success if you can't help the next person in line? Especially when that person is a friend, a good friend, and that good friend needs help.

There was nothing else left to do. We would have to sell the house. There was a little equity available so we could release that, pay off Farid, and still have some left over to invest in a new business. It was still unknown, but that was our only option. Oh, and we would rent for a while until we got back on our feet. You see? A plan. Everything looks better with a plan.

Time to look for a Realtor.

20

British Delicious

Florida Realtors are another breed. The majority of them are ladies and most of them promote themselves with pictures that are older than God's dog. 80s Dynasty-style photos have never gone out of fashion in the Florida Real Estate world; heck, you would think shoulder pads were still a thing. I did say the majority. Let me introduce you to the other 10%; no-nonsense, hard-hitting Terry Tillung. She would get your house sold for you, no questions asked. She told us what we had to do to the house to get it sold, we did it, and it sold. Simple. Real Estate 101. Little did we know at the time, but this was to be the only home we ever owned in Florida.

The next phase of rentals was a little weird. It was through a friend of a friend who lived in Canada but owned a nice home in Cobb's Landing, of all places. This was the nicer part, to be known as The Bell's house. We already knew they were selling their home the following year, but it was available for nine months which suited us. After all, by that stage we should have enough credit history to buy our own place, as long as we could get a deposit together, which seemed achievable if we stayed on our current trajectory.

There was a small caveat with this rental, however. The owners had already rented it out for about three weeks during our nine months, which meant we had to find somewhere temporary to stay during this time. To make matters worse, it was the same time Vanessa's mum was visiting from the UK. The only saving grace was that we had rented it fully furnished, all we had to move out was our clothes. All our other belongings were in storage. By now I already had PODS on speed dial,in fact I still do to this day. We found two small waterfront units adjacent to each other in Dunedin which would become our temporary home for the month, sort of like a vacation from a vacation, but it worked out fine and before we knew it we were back at the Bell's house. Side note: for a home to make it onto our all-time Rental board, it has to be for a minimum of one month. Therefore, the Bell's house and the Dunedin Rental officially became Rentals #3 and #4.

This seaways us nicely to house number five, also known as the red house. It was a nice size with a pool, but very old-fashioned inside. However, it was a bargain at $1900 a month. We had nice neighbours and lived in a cul-de-sac, so it was super quiet. The main things that spring to mind about this home are all wildlife related, such as having a baby moccasin snake swimming in the pool. We had to get someone to "harvest" that, whereas I had to harvest the big-ass wolf spider in the kitchen myself. It was done very unprofessionally and, I apologise now, probably not very quickly. Well, it was as quick as it took to paralyse it with a whole can of bug spray and then karate chop it numerous times with a broom handle. Done, or so I thought. Look away now if you are squeamish: she was pregnant, I only found out after as all the little baby spiders came into view. I am sorry; I don't like spiders, and Vanessa hates spiders. I had no choice.

Anyway, the red house was going to be a stepping stone to bigger and better things. The kids were settled in school, both playing volleyball in their spare time. Tali was in a nice Montessori school run by a very nice English lady, and Vanessa and I were hatching plans for our new business. By this time, we had also discovered the benefits of leasing a car. In a nutshell, we could sell one of our cars...mine was chosen, my beautiful Infiniti FX35 I might add...and replace it with just one monthly payment. There were no maintenance costs and we could just pocket the money we got for my car, which was a little long in the tooth and would start needing money spent on it soon. Ring a bell? It was the same deal as the house. When it starts costing you money, sell it! It is a great philosophy in theory, but eventually you end up with no possessions you actually own. Apparently. I can't imagine that ever happening to anyone.

Anyway, we found a guy in Tarpon that would put the car in his showroom and take a percentage when it sold. Sounds too good to be true? Yes, it was. Another theme is starting here: the crooks are always bigger in America. Apparently, he could only get x amount for the car and asked if we were happy to accept that. It was just before Christmas and the money came in handy, so we said yes. We got a check, eventually, and thought nothing more of it until the new owner rang us to ask us something about the car. I joked that they got a bargain at the price we sold it for, but the new owner assured me he had paid over $2000 more for the car. It appears the dealer pocketed the $2000 on top of the 10% we already paid him. I called after the winter break but couldn't get hold of him. I was the least of his worries. It turns out he had done it to countless people before and the police were about to swing by and charge him with fraud. I never got my $2000 back, but he did get a long stretch behind bars, which he rightly deserved.

There's a little mini fraud for you right there. Lightning couldn't strike twice, could it? We had what was left of the equity from the house and a slightly reduced lump sum from the sale of my car. Did I mention it was an Infiniti FX35, white, leather seats, and fast? Best car I ever had! Anyway, that was gone and we had a swish new Ford Explorer on lease. Time to invest.

For the whole time we had been living in Florida and even before when we came on vacation, sorry, holiday, we loved Dunedin and all its Scottish heritage. There was one little shop just off the Main Street that was full of character. We heard rumours it would be available soon and we got ourselves to the top of the list as potential renters. At the time it was being run as a small coffee gift shop with a side helping of Mystic Meg; *Uber eclectic*. We negotiated a lease and started working on what was to become "British Delicious," a space that would celebrate all things British. By all things, we meant all things: British football, curry nights, British cover bands, Boddingtons Ale, full English breakfasts, and Cream Teas.

Now, you might be saying to yourself right about now that it sounds like a lot, and you'd be right. The lovely Vanessa just wanted to concentrate on breakfast, tea, coffee, afternoon tea, and sandwiches, including the soon-to-be famous Coronation Chicken. This was the right decision. The wrong decision was to go with what I wanted, which was basically everything! I thought the more we did, the more people would come and the more money we would make. In theory, that should work, in my mind. Reality was we spread ourselves too thin and had to work too many hours. I loved doing the live music outside. We had both an interior and exterior bar, and the building itself was full of character. It was a beautiful building but haunted. I found myself working until eleven or twelve at the weekend and then having to be back at 7:30 to open up for breakfast. It wasn't uncommon for me to work 90 to 100 hours a week.

We were also a bit shortsighted when it came to our marketing and the message we were trying to get over. Back in Wales, we had been at the forefront of all things branding. Some was very subtle, but it all came together to create the perfect brand experience. What we found in the US was that you can be too clever for your own good. The sign was simple. It just read what the shop was, a "does exactly what it says on the tin" type mentality. A launderette would have a big sign saying launderette because it was a launderette. "Loads of Fun" or "The Spin Doctor" would have been far too clever for your average American. A hardware store would simply have "Hardware" over the door, not "Level Up Hardware." You get the gist.

Anyway, we sort of didn't get the memo and it has never been in our style to be mundane, so we ran with British Deli-Cious. The amount of locals coming in thinking it was a deli, in the American sense of a deli, was amazing. They were expecting curated meats, cheeses, and all things Charcuterie. They didn't hang around when they realised it was a glorified greasy spoon with warm beer, fancy tablecloths, and soccer. Our British following did grow, however. They were won

          SIXTY NOT OUT

over by our cream teas, bacon sandwiches, and our wit, charm, and humour. Curry nights on a Friday were popular and we even hosted a few psychic nights which were very popular, even with the dead as they visited on many occasions, or so I'm told. It was without doubt haunted. It had that eerie vibe last thing at night as I was closing up. I'm not a true believer, but there was definitely something there that made me leave in a hurry! In a hurry for a curry.. that would have been a great take-out idea for our curries. There's one we missed.

It all started to get a little tedious. We made adequate money and we definitely broke even, but a mix of the economy, our location, and our uniqueness limited our potential. It was also very hard work with long hours and lots of paperwork for wages which was a ball-ache. I compared everything to Footprints: only open in season, minimal paperwork, and large amounts of fun. Now I had 12 months of work a year, lots of red tape, and way too many long days. One blessing was Ali, who was an English girl full of energy, enthusiasm, and funny in a rude sort of way. Most of the customers loved her, and the ones that didn't I ended up serving. However, the realisation that I was missing out on seeing the girls grow up and the fact that Vanessa needed to be home to look after them meant I saw less and less of them. It was almost like a Wylfa withdrawal from public sight for Vanessa, but now she had a valid reason.

I also knew our time was almost up when I found myself dreading our regular customer coming in at 10:30 every morning, ordering a drip coffee, handing over $2.14 exactly with no tip, and standing at the counter expecting me to entertain him. It was hard work. You know who you are, Mark. It was similar, once again, to standing behind the bar in the Wylfa listening to some boring plumber go on and on about something painfully uninteresting all while drinking a half a bitter at the pace of a snail. Not that snails drink bitter, of course; I heard they are more partial to wine.

I mean, we had some light relief. I'm very proud that we managed to put on a fabulous wedding reception for a couple; we provided food and drinks and they were beyond happy. Definitely something we are proud of. The only other light relief that springs to mind during the two-plus years we ran the store was when I wasn't there. I managed to get a cool modelling job in Martinique for their tourist board. It was a name-dropper's delight. We were taking pictures in Bryan Adam's house, which was next door to Tommy Hilfiger's house. We did some shots in Princess Margaret's old home and had lunch at Mick Jagger's favourite spot, to name but a few. I also slept in the same room Gisele Bundchen was staying in the week before. All very A-list, and then there was me!

The most stressful time of the whole trip was the airport, well, not really the airport, which was a bamboo hut, but the small plane that we had to use to get on and off the island. It was very Indiana Jones. It went up and down extremely quickly and was extremely noisy; those propellers don't half make a racket. Strangely it felt safe, unlike the time I was flying into Glasgow on another modelling gig, this time for Slaters Menswear. I was sitting behind Jon Snow of Channel 4 news fame, known for not only that but for his outrageously colourful socks he used to wear. I remember that day did not disappoint; we almost made the news ourselves that day for nearly all the wrong reasons. We were flying through an electrical storm and we got hit by a bolt of lightning. It all happened very quickly, but it seemed to last forever. In those moments life slows down and you are able to analyse everything in the greatest detail. I remember a bang, a flash of light that travelled down the whole length of the plane, and then darkness and silence. We dropped what must have been a few hundred feet and then, as if by magic or divine intervention, the lights came back on, I heard the engines again, and we levelled out. You know it's a big thing when even the stewardesses looked nervous, and they looked nervous.

Okay, here I am rambling on about a flight to Glasgow when I need to get back to British Delicious in Dunedin, Florida. I'm a huge believer that life is a journey. It's not about the destination, it's about how you get there, and decisions you make on that journey could lead you to a different destination. All you can do is make decisions in the moment with the facts that are available to you at that time, as has been the case in our lives. One thing always starts to fizzle out but, before it goes completely, it gives us a clear indication of what's next. This was the case here. We were exhausted and just making ends meet when I got a surprise visit from a Realtor whose business cards we had on the counter. She was English

　　　　SIXTY NOT OUT

and she brought me a bottle of whisky. She didn't know me well enough to know I didn't do the whisky thing, but it was a nice gesture. She went on to thank me for all the business she had gotten from me handing out her cards. Dunedin was popular and she was selling many houses to holidaymakers that fell in love with the town.

That night Vanessa and I discussed the possibility of trying to sell the business if the opportunity came around and, based on the conversation with the whisky-giving agent, I decided I should pursue a career in Real Estate myself. It was decided that was the path we would take. Low and behold, the very next day, one of our regular English customers came in and said if ever we were considering selling the business, they would be interested. If ever you wanted a sign, there it was! We negotiated back and forth a little on the details and cleared with the owner that it would be alright if we left, which it was. We put the wheels in motion and before you knew it, we were out and I turned my attention to studying for the Real Estate License, which was not as easy as I thought it would be and a lot more time-consuming.

We really hadn't made any money from selling the business. We just managed to get out and cover all our expenses. The real win for us was the fact we had freed up a lot of spare time; time to spend with each other and with the kids. I had missed out over the last two years or so. I was determined to chill for a while, get some quality family time under my belt, and eventually turn my attention to buying and selling homes for other people, not ourselves unfortunately.

Over our time in the US, we have noticed a series of patterns that would play out regularly, with most of them being negative. We were just about to experience another one of these patterns, the pattern known as: just as you settle in a house, start planning for your future, feel secure, your landlord decides he wants to sell the house sort of pattern. Sound familiar? Maybe not yet, but I can assure you it will! This is when I throw in the "every cloud has a silver lining" quote. Luckily, just prior to learning this news and after three months of studying, I managed to pass the Real Estate Exam, which meant I had a value proposition I could make to our landlord.

I had just closed my first deal which was a commercial space for a friend of ours. I had ended up hanging my license with another friend of ours who was a broker after my first brokerage said I couldn't do the commercial deal myself. So I switched, saved myself a chunk of commission, and was now a lone wolf working for a small independent company, calling my own shots. The plan was for me to list the house and for us to live in the home right up until the day before closing, thus enabling the landlord to realise the maximum amount of rent and for us to have a place to live right up until a day before we didn't! He liked the plan.

We went for it.

21

HSN

Just as my Real Estate career was starting off, I was fortunate to also have the opportunity to indulge in something else I had been looking into for a while. It is also something many people had said I would be good at, so if the chance came then, why not? Home Shopping Network, here we go!

My HSN journey began in a similar fashion to most things in my life: a natural progression. I've always had secret career desires and ambitions which I tend to keep to myself but work towards every day. If I don't get there then so be it, but I will do everything in my power to make them a reality. That was the case with HSN. All through my modelling journey in the US, the enigma of HSN has always been there. I've worked with numerous people who always said, "Hey, you'd be great on HSN, why don't you try out?"

I have always been extremely comfortable in front of a camera, both still photography and video. Most of the video work I've done has been recorded, if you screw up you can always go again. The only real time I struggle is if there is a script and I have to memorise more than two lines at a time. That is a big-time struggle, and again I blame the overuse of recreational drugs in my younger years. The beauty of HSN, as I perceived it, was that there was no script, so how could I mess up? Just hit a few bullet points while ad-libbing and goof around the rest of the time. Sign me up!

The difficulty was getting me in front of someone there who could assess my potential and determine whether I would be a good fit. I managed to get contact details for someone in production from a friend and I emailed them my resume and a little about my background. I feel like I might have leaned on my catering background a little too strongly, because a few weeks later I got a call to come in and do an audition for the kitchen department. Pots and pans, if I remember correctly.

The day comes and I breeze in all confident; some natural confidence but the majority was fake confidence. You know: fake it till you make it. I do believe I felt quite confident. Well, that didn't last long. The first thing they had me do was slice a cucumber as fast as I could, just like the chefs do on TV. It was strange, that it's almost like they were looking for a chef on TV. Chop, chop, chop: very fast, very accurate, very professional. Now, I could chop cucumber for my sandwiches, but I could not chop it to the standard they were looking for. It was very stop-start and the slices were of a very irregular size. Believe it or not, I didn't get that gig, but I was in the system and I was now about to work that system to my advantage. Once I had my in, I was like a pig at a tater!

I emailed back and made some excuse about my poor cucumber chopping, but said if any other options came in I was open to auditioning. Now I don't know what happened next, but I sort of skipped forward a couple of steps and, before I knew it, I was scheduled with the on-air trainer to learn and practise techniques before being allowed to go live. It is almost like someone at HSN took a shine to me and fast-tracked me to the front of the line.

I did my training. It didn't fill me with much confidence as I always felt about 80% happy with my performances. I struggled with coordination, which camera I was on, and listening to the producers in my earpiece, which is pretty much all there is. Safe to say, I struggled with all of it! I'm sure my enthusiasm carried me through, that and a large sprinkling of my accent.

SIXTY NOT OUT

I started going to production meetings for HSN's own brand, Improvements: lots of little gadgety-type things that they would air at random times throughout the day. Without really getting any official notice, I just sort of slid into the role of male on-air guest for the Improvements range. Nice. I faked it and I made it, in this context anyway.

Now, don't get me wrong, this was by no stretch of the imagination a regular gig. It was very sporadic. I had a few late-night small segments, maybe three or four minutes at a time, but it was fun. I wasn't nervous and just rode off my adrenaline. I remember a couple of days we had Improvements specials where we had numerous products lined up throughout different studios that me and the female presenter would have to showcase, with the help of the regular host, of course. That was the most fun: just bouncing between studios, running on set for a quick five- or six-minute demo, then a break and an hour or so later doing it all again. It really was fun. Unfortunately, HSN were winding down the Improvements side of their business, a decision that was made before I came along, I can assure you. That's what they said, anyway.

The work slowed down, but a few opportunities opened up with other products. What was good was that the casting department at HSN now had a showreel of me they sent out to any potential vendors looking to hire an on-air talent with an English accent. Who knows what opportunities would present themselves!

If I'm honest, not many did. I worked with a company that made portable AC units, one that made an electric fire that made crackling sounds and had lights inside which made it look authentic. I was an ambassador for a water filtration company that had huge potential, but ultimately the product was sub-standard so that fizzled out. My favourite of all was a company who made pre-lit fake Christmas Trees in various sizes. It had about 40 different light options: very cool. I also got to fly up to Pennsylvania to their offices for the day to learn about the product. We did a daily special with the trees in the run-up to Christmas which means we were on air for a full 24 hours. We weren't on constantly, but we appeared about every couple of hours or would do a 20-30 minute presentation.

That was the pinnacle for me: no sleep and running on pure nervous energy. I think their sales were solid also, which was always nice to hear.

I had hoped to do it the following year, but I heard they had been let down by a supplier and that they had no choice but to go out of business. Around the same time, I felt a shift in my attitude to the shows. Whereas before I would only get a little nervous but use that energy to carry me through the presentation, I was now finding that the nerves and apprehension were becoming overwhelming and they would affect my confidence. The more nervous I got, the more I would question my ability and that would directly impact my performance. There is only so much breathing in the coffee and blowing out the candles one man can do behind the scenes. It was a downward spiral that was becoming very overwhelming. I no longer enjoyed the thought of going live on air and I would find excuses to not be available for some shows and also distance myself from some of the vendors I worked with. I had done a complete 180.

Whether this was a realization that my confidence was gone, the fact that I didn't feel happy about my performances, or external factors that were at play, I did not know. It was probably a combination of all three, but as Covid hit and all the live shows were paused and preference went to hosts who had a home studio set-up. I was not one of those hosts. I had the perfect opportunity to slip away into the shadows. I loved my time at HSN, but I know now that it's done, especially with the relocation to the QVC studios in Pennsylvania. I would never change it and I'm happy I fulfilled a dream that I had. After all, that's what life is all about: having a dream, realising it, and moving on when the time is right. And the time was right.

That's not to say I wouldn't pick up the phone if they rang today! Never say never, right?

    SIXTY NOT OUT

22

The Real, Real Estate Story

By spring 2015, we were sort of in a plateau state. I was just starting out on my Real Estate journey, Vanessa had established a business called *GOT Jewelery*, the kids were doing well in school, and the Volvo was still running. We had agreed with the owners of the red house that we would list their home whilst still living in it. It was a bit awkward with showings, but the commission I would earn helped us get over that.

I guess by now you could class us as comfortable. We didn't live an extravagant life, not by choice but more because we couldn't afford to, but as a unit we were tight. We were living a typical middle-class life: not much excitement, but we had each other and that seemed to be enough. The Jay Peak thing was still a little concerning. The quarterly checks were minimal when we received them and there were online rumours starting to spread that all was not well. Typical of me, I sort of put my head in the sand and hoped they would go away. Besides, what was I going to do that would change anything? If this was a thing, then it would play out with or without any input from me.

I managed to get the house under contract, which was amazing from my professional standpoint, but from the family standpoint it sort of sucked. It meant we had to pack up again, change addresses again on all our accounts, change ID, forward all mail, and come up with first, last, and deposit on our new rental, which is basically three times the monthly rent. It was a big chunk of change, but luckily I was getting a bigger chunk of change in commission from the house sale. It is funny how things like that seem to happen.

Now, once again, as had happened many times before, fate rode in on a white horse and saved the day. As was becoming a lucrative theme for me, I happened to get one of my other listings under contract at the same time. Now, this lovely lady had already vacated her townhome in Palm Harbor for a new life in The Villages, which is an active retirement community north of us. It is also rumoured to be a bit of a swinging community as well. I don't think that is in their brochure, but the reputation has grown over the years. I also don't think my seller was a prime candidate either, as she was in her late seventies already and didn't look capable of swinging a cat, let alone anything else. However, I'm not one to judge. It will be interesting to see what I'm like in twenty years! It might make a good book in the future, if I survive that long. So she was away doing whatever she was doing and she was kind enough to let us stay at her old place until we could find somewhere else. We put our things into storage, PODS to the rescue, and made Anne's townhome our townhome for four or five weeks until my buyer moved in. Anne's townhome is now officially classed as Rental #6.

While we have been fortunate on many occasions to have referrals just land in our lap when we least expect it, the opposite has also been true on a much greater level. I have had moments where I actually assume that someone is going to use me as their Realtor, or their actions suggest I am already working for them, only for the rug to be pulled out from underneath when I least expect it or, more importantly, when I am relying on that commission for survival. It is another one of life's "what ifs".

One thing I have learned in this checkered Real Estate journey of mine is never assume! It can, and does, lead to a lot of disappointment and can test relationships to the max, both with friends and acquaintances as well as family. Many times I have mistakenly assumed someone would use me as their agent

     SIXTY NOT OUT

only to find out, usually via social media, that they have indeed moved forward, but not with me. Buyers are liars; not all the time, but enough to test friendships. There are only so many times you can smile at someone through gritted teeth before you just stop smiling at them. It definitely helps you to streamline those emotions. In the long run, it's my family I take it out on. I can be moody and short-tempered for a while, but then, as if by magic, another opportunity presents itself and all is good with the world; for a while, anyway. I am learning, and have learned, to be a lot more direct with people now. It's easier to find out early on that they don't want to work with you than farther down the line when I've already invested time and money. Either way it stings, but honesty really is the best policy. Honesty from day one is vital, as after all, this is my livelihood and I take it really seriously, and so does my family.

One day, while helping Vanessa at an event in Dunedin, I took the bold step of walking into the office of Coastal Properties, a big player in the world of boutique brokerages. I asked if I could join them and explained that I wanted to take my business to the next level. I didn't meet the minimum requirement for business sales but, thanks to my suave English accent, they said they would consider it. They said they would let me know soon. On walking back to Vanessa, my phone rang and I answered. Apparently, it was the final step of the interview process: if I answered, I could join them, and if I didn't, then probably not. I had obeyed the first rule of Real Estate: if your phone rings, answer it!

I'm glad I did because this would be the start of almost ten happy years with them. Well, probably nine happy and one not so, but we'll get to that. 2015 turned out to be a good year and 2016 started off amazing. Vanessa found us a lovely home in Crystal Beach to move into, one which we could see ourselves possibly buying at some stage. I had it written into the lease that we would be given the first option if they ever decided to sell. We were sitting pretty. We had a lovely home, Rental #7, The Yellow House. The kids were good, the wife was good, Cookie was good, and the Volvo was still going.

The house wasn't 100% ideal. I mean, the pool was a little small and the concrete floors throughout were crippling on your feet, but the kitchen, front porch, and double-sided open fireplace more than made up for it. One small problem we had to overcome was it was only a three-bedroom home and we really needed four. Both the older girls had grown out of sharing and quite rightly needed their own space and privacy. Tali was still at the age where, if she could, she would still choose to sleep in our room. Unfortunately, the lack of space in our bedroom and the concrete floor made that a non-starter. There was one option left, and before I explain to you what it is, I want you to know that Tali was 100% on board with it, so don't be calling any child services on us. After all, she was six, and who messes with a six-year-old!

Here goes: our bedroom had two closets. I know, I know. One was a decent size, the other was even bigger, almost bedroom size for a small person. It had a door, a light, and air conditioning, and a mattress fit in there perfectly. There was no space around the outside, but it fit perfectly. Also, all around the walls above were hanging rails, which meant she slept under all her lovely dresses and t-shirts. It was just like a princess room. We told her it was just like a princess's room and she agreed; she was genuinely happy. As long as she had "Dirty Baby," she was happy. Before you ask, Dirty Baby was, and is, her plushie. Anyway, bedroom number four was solved.

We decided we were in a good place. Our experience of renting up until that time had been, on the whole, a positive experience. We were working towards ownership again and if we had to skimp and save a little along the way, then so be it. I had already started to talk to the owner about buying the house and we had agreed on a price. Our credit history was strong and the line we had been sold by Jay Peak...that they would initiate an exit strategy after five years of investment... was due to mature. They would soon be telling us how they intended to repay the money. That was our deposit right there, and then some!

After all the turmoil and stress of the previous years, things were definitely on the up. We had a positive outlook and our future looked bright, that is until April 12th, 2016. On April 12th, 2016, everything changed.

     SIXTY NOT OUT

23

Jay Peak

Where to start? We've got pre-April 12th 2016 and post. Up until now we have only dealt with the pre, so let's summarise that. As I look back now, nearly eighteen years later, I struggle to find anything we would have done differently. I felt like our due diligence was comprehensive. We researched extensively, made phone calls, spent hours online down the proverbial rabbit hole, and even visited our immigration attorney to go through the whole structure of everything. I mean, it was the only EB-5 offering that was overseen and audited by state regulators. State approved. It was touted as the poster child of the EB-5 world, and to us there was no other option.

We didn't go into it blind, maybe just a little blinkered. It would enable us to live anywhere in the US. We would be free to work anywhere in the US, and it was a path to green cards and ultimately citizenship. We would get a free vacation at the resort every year, and a quarterly percentage of operating profits once the resort was fully operational. An exit strategy would be implemented after five years, involving selling off the resort. A very neat package, all for $500,000.

Too good to be true? Of course it was. We should have walked away right then, but we had progressed far enough down the application route that walking away did not seem to be a viable option. Our crazy, young, adventurous spirit told us to go for it. We had been blessed with financial good fortune previously, so why wouldn't this just be a continuation of that happy trip to the top of the money tree?

Because life happens. Just when you think you are invincible, it has a way of shaking that money tree and bringing you back down to earth with one almighty thump.

There had been rumours and gossip for a while that all was not well on the Jay Peak front. A few of the attorneys they used to process applications and facilitate the immigration paperwork were questioning the validity of the numbers coming out of Jay Peak. One attorney in particular wrote to one hundred other attorneys telling them he was terminating his relationship with Jay Peak because he could no longer trust what Jay Peak was telling him. This was the same company I had chatted to during our initial due diligence, someone whose opinion I trusted. It was early 2012, and we hadn't been in the US for even two years. This was worrying.

Jay Peak pushed back and commissioned an "independent" review of everything, which obviously found no wrongdoing. Coincidentally, not long after that review we received the biggest quarterly cheque we had ever had. I wanted to believe everything was as it should be. I was looking for the smallest possible signs everything was okay, and the financial review, doubled with the nice cheque, helped alleviate those worries somewhat. You always have to look for the positive, right? They always seem easier to find when you really need them.

That was the first warning sign. The second was the lack of consistency with the quarterly payments. One would be skipped completely with the promise it would be rolled into the next one. Whichever way you sliced the cake, the total at the end of the year was getting smaller and smaller until, sometime in 2015, it stopped altogether.

   SIXTY NOT OUT

Up until now I have referred to Jay Peak just as the name of the resort we invested in. Time to introduce you to the two main characters in this whole scandal: Mr Bill Stenger and Mr Ariel Quiros. I use the term mister under advisement.

Stenger was the face of everything, the Vermonter who did good, always rubbing shoulders with the political upper class, Bernie Sanders and Peter Shumlin and the like. Quiros, not so much. I think he was the mastermind behind it all, the driving force on the business side from day one, and ultimately the face of the demise of the Jay Peak we had invested in. In my opinion he looks like a rogue, he ended up fitting that description perfectly.

There we were, relatively comfortable in the Yellow House, also affectionately known as Number Six. Wife, kids, animals and the Volvo were all good. Plans were in place to buy Number Six. Normal morning. Dog walk, coffee, check emails, still half asleep. Not for long.

I cannot exactly remember how I was notified or how I came to hear about it, but there it was in black and white, no disputing. The SEC had frozen all assets of Jay Peak and placed it in receivership. I read it once, twice. Googled what that actually meant, and read it a third time.

My heart started beating at a hundred miles an hour and fell to the pit of my stomach at the same time, if that is possible. I can honestly say that at that moment the speed at which our world was ripped out from underneath us was overwhelming. I felt hollow. I felt angry. I felt confused. I felt helpless, very helpless. Our future as we knew it changed in that split second. Gone was the security, gone were the dreams of owning a home again, and although I did not realise it at the time, gone was my self confidence, my positivity and my fun loving personality. It would take years for me to acknowledge that, but looking back now I know that was the start of a depression that would last years and is still lingering to this day.

Instantly, Ness could see it in my face. The fact that all the blood had rushed out was probably a giveaway. I'm sure she initially thought it was a death I had just learned about, which in reality it was. The death of our happily ever after. There was no point in sugar coating it. Our $550,000 had gone, and the chances of getting it back were at best poor and at worst, we were never seeing that moolah again. Once a receiver gets involved, then we are talking years for things to get settled. All that litigation and all those billing hours can get charged to someone else's dime. Payday for the attorneys.

Side note. Nearly ten years later and the receiver is still doing his thing. Extremely time consuming and ridiculously lucrative for him.

Just to clarify, our day-to-day life did not change overnight. I was still earning a decent living in real estate. It is just that our dreams and desires for the future changed. It had a huge knock on effect. I appreciate everyone goes through life changing situations every day and one could say that if I can still provide food and shelter for my family then I should just be grateful, because I am aware there are a lot of people out there struggling with the basics who would swap places with me in a heartbeat. I am not belittling their situation. I am just telling the story from my perspective, and from my perspective our whole focus had to change. This was not going to be something that was just going to go away. Every day, week, month, eventually turning into years, the anger, sadness and guilt just kept growing inside me. I became more withdrawn, quieter, and my confidence fell through the floor.

I was angry that this had happened to us. I was sad we would not be able to provide the life I felt my family deserved. I was guilty because ultimately it was my name on the Jay Peak application. We had torn our kids away from an idyllic life in Wales with the promise of better things, to follow the American Dream, only to be betrayed by a few individuals who interpreted the American Dream differently.

The immediate consequence was we would not be able to buy House Number Six because we could not get the down payment. I remember a very emotional David going for a meeting with the owner, explaining our situation and looking for sympathy or for him to give us some sort of break, which was not forthcoming. Unfortunately the emotion turned to anger and we called an abrupt end to the meeting before I got us evicted. The next day I apologised and he was gracious but still adamant that if we could not buy the house then he still needed to sell it to someone else.

I tried the old trick of selling it for him while we were still tenants, the old maximising rental income trick, but that did not work. He would let me try to sell it unofficially for the first month, if I could not find a buyer then he was going to give the listing to friends of his. Everyone has a friend who is a Realtor, right?

Not surprisingly, with no marketing, no MLS and no sign, I was not able to pull a buyer out of my ass in the four weeks. The listing went to his friends and the clock started ticking. Once a buyer was found, we were out. Time to look for Rental Number Seven, just the first of many consequences that the Jay Peak scam would force upon us.

Mentally I was now in limbo. Conservative estimates were that the whole receivership thing would last six or seven years at least until it was resolved. We were in it for the long haul. Little did I know how completely overwhelming it would be. First we had to find another roof to put over our heads, and luckily we found a place in Tarpon. This too was yellow, but as we had already used up the yellow house name with Number Seven, this one would be known as The Tarpon House, Number Eight. It was owned by an ex French international rugby player, and the agent was also French. Given our school day French was very rusty, it is amazing we managed to negotiate a deal, but we did. Physically we were sound, mentally, not so much.

I am very much aware now that any corporate litigation goes about as fast as a snail. In fact, if you entered corporate litigation into a snail race, I am convinced it would finish last. At the time, however, in the early days of the saga, I was under the misguided hope that things might move along a little quicker than they did.

I joined lots of forums made up of fellow Jay Peakers who had been wronged. There was so much information swirling around it was difficult to decipher what was true and what was not. The only reliable source of information was the official website set up by the receiver, which would post relevant information when it became available.

With my hand on my heart, I tell you that I checked that website three times every day for eight years. I constantly had a page open on my phone in Safari just on that page. To say it completely took over my life would be accurate. I am not saying I did not function as a human as well, but it was always there, lurking in the background, ready to jump out and suffocate me the moment anything negative happened in another aspect of my life. Sometimes it did not need a reason to come out. It would just be there from the moment I woke up to the last thing I thought about as I lay down to sleep. It would completely consume me some days.

Subconsciously, I think the whole scam took over ten percent of my brain, limiting my capacity to be happy, limiting my creativity, destroying my self confidence, and tempering any excitement I might have about life. It stole a lot of my joy for a long time.

You do not get those years back, and I now feel bitter that I let it dictate so much of my mood. But at the time I did not have the mental strength to shake off the negativity. I just accepted it, and that is such a waste.

The next few years followed a pattern. It was almost as if we were on autopilot. I was numb to the outside world, functioning on eighty percent capacity, semi reclusive. My bubble had popped.

The French owners of the Tarpon House, or should that be La Maison Tarpon, decided they wanted to sell, no surprise there. We lined up rental Number Nine in Dunedin, Tiverton Court. We would be secure there for as long as we wanted, as the Californian owners had no intention of selling. They were going to retire there in five or six years. Perfect. So we all moved in, minus the

SIXTY NOT OUT

Volvo. Unfortunately the Volvo was no more. She had been part exchanged by this stage as both the older girls were now driving. Luckily they had not inherited their mother's reversing and parking skills, but just as worrying they had not inherited my skill for driving slowly. That is a whole different story.

In the great scale of life, Tiverton Court was very mundane. Highlights included a snake in the bathroom, the cats bringing numerous body parts of rabbits, geckos and frogs into the house, and, of course, the owners changing their minds and deciding to sell the house. No surprise there.

We had found a little life rhythm, as we always do just before we have to move. It is like someone is watching and thinks, wow, those Woodings are starting to look a little comfortable there, almost happy some might say, let's just throw a little spanner in the works. Let's have them move house again.

The Jay Peak thing was still there, always in the background. Its ugly head did not raise itself quite as often. This was helped by the fact I had joined a couple of class action lawsuits, and they seemed as though they might be somewhat successful somewhere down the line. At least we were hearing positive noises from the attorneys, however small that was, I was going to latch onto it.

Through all of our turmoil and all the moving, there is one thing that remains constant, that is the five of us. The family. Our love never wavered. In fact, in adversity it became stronger. Ever since Day One in the US we have had this unwritten bond that it is us against the world. That is one positive we can take from this whole fiasco. The fact we are stronger than we knew, and that no matter what, through all the shit life can throw at you, we still have each other. Solid.

So we moved again. Margaret Way, Number Ten, again in Dunedin. Gated community, nice pool, big house, all five of us. A truthful landlord who promised he had absolutely no desire to sell. Let us see how long that lasts.

We were surviving, bumping along the bottom I like to call it, breaking even if you will. We have always said that when things look really dire, something miraculously pops up to ensure we can keep going for a little longer. Be under no illusion, there have been times, far too many times, we have been down to our last few hundred dollars. Make no mistake, during our whole time here we have never been in a position to put any money aside, to save anything. It has been feast or famine. That is real estate for you. We have always had to rely on the income we make from our self employed endeavours. No corporate America here with fancy pensions and benefits. To balance the freedom of being an entrepreneur you have to make a few sacrifices, and a steady reliable income is one of those sacrifices.

I still have not worked out our calling. I know we were meant to come here for something, whether for Vanessa and I or for one of the kids. There has to be a reason. I do not think we have found it yet, but the fact the universe conspires to keep us here by providing opportunity or money when we need it most convinces me that our journey is not quite over. Sometimes it has been decisions we made ourselves to keep the wolf from the door, like cashing in my small pension when I had the choice, or stepping out of the box to epoxy resin a friend's garage and paint his house just to get a few grand to pay the rent that month and put some food on the table. Thank you YouTube for teaching me how to do that. At times we have had to step up. Other times things just landed at our feet, giving us the ability to make it through the next few months.

Covid is a prime example. Terrible time for everyone, but it came at a time when real estate was going through a lull and money was tight. Being self employed, we could file for unemployment, which saved our bacon for a few months. Then, lo and behold, real estate in Florida went crazy for two years. Things just had a way of perpetuating our stay here.

We had also started to get a few small settlements from the Jay Peak receivership. Some of the litigation was being finalized, some companies settled prior to having to go to court as the scale of the fraud became apparent, and a lot of companies who were complicit did not want their good name dragged out for public consultation. They settled out of court, paid the big money while not admitting to any guilt or wrongdoing. We all know they were guilty as fuck. Why pay the money if you are innocent? Crazy way of getting out of things. We are not guilty, but why do you not take all this money and let us make it go away?

This momentum really helped with my overall mood of restrained positivity. Things were definitely on the up. Work was good. The family was good. We were getting positive noises about Jay Peak litigation and we even had a new puppy. Criminal charges against Stenger and Quiros and two other nobodies were filed on top of the civil cases, which was the cherry on the cake. They could all rot in prison for all I cared.

You do not have to be a rocket scientist to know what is coming now. It is not just one time. This is a double smackdown.

After struggling with his health for a while, my dad passed away in March 2022. All financial worries seem irrelevant and inconsequential when stacked up against family. Your health and the health of your family are paramount. The moment I heard the news I went straight into a sort of grief fog. All other noise stops. It is like your body goes into protection mode and shuts everything else down so you can concentrate on what is important. It is like everything is moving in slow motion and the sound is reduced to fifty percent with a light fuzz over everything. I know that sounds crazy, but if you have been through it, maybe it makes sense.

Anyway, that is one way of cutting out the Jay Peak noise, and it definitely worked for a month or two.

We were on our way back from my dad's funeral in the UK on a layover in Atlanta when I got a call that would jolt me back into reality with a bang. The landlord of Margaret Way, Number Ten, decided he wanted to sell his house. You cannot make this shit up, right?

No more brain fog or fifty percent fuzzy sound. Time to focus. Welcome back to America. Time for us to kick you in the balls again.

After the initial gut wrenching feeling of having to move again had subsided, my mind switched to "is there any opportunity in this for me?" That was short lived. I floated the idea of selling the house for him while we still lived there. I even shared the success story from the red house and emphasised the fact that the owner there was getting paid rent up until the day it was sold. It all fell on deaf ears. Paired with the fact he had already lined up a Realtor, I really had no chance. The clock was ticking once again. This time we had six weeks to find somewhere else, which was fifty percent more than we normally got.

Time to mix a little more confusion into our headspace. At this particular moment we were definitely weighing up the distinct possibility that we would buy this time around. There were positives, mainly financial. Jay Peak was for sale and rumours were abound it would be sold before year end. The private litigation we were involved with regarding the fraud was also going through an uptick in positivity. The words "make whole" had been used a couple of times on phone calls. In layman's terms, we might get all our money back. I was also going through a productive phase in real estate. All very positive. It was also at the back of my mind that eventually I would get some inheritance from my dad.

The only real negative was the market had gone through a ridiculous price increase and homes were now fifty percent more than they were eighteen months ago, so affordability was an issue.

It was decided we would try to wait a while, see if we could consolidate a little with the hope that in a few months things would be clearer. After all, it had only been a few months since my dad passed, we did not want to do anything too radical.

We decided to take a six month fully furnished rental in Safety Harbor until the dust had settled. For recording purposes, we are now at Rental Number Eleven, the Safety Harbor Cottage. This was everything. Loads of character, modern throughout and walkable to downtown. A perfect place to take a moment and regroup.

Apart from the sadness of losing my dad, everything else seemed to be steady. We had a little money behind us with the prospect of more to come. I should have been able to see that the positives completely outweighed the negatives. My family was good. We were all healthy. We were living in a nice place and

   SIXTY NOT OUT

we were sound financially. The only negative was the grief I was feeling for my dad. Looking back now, I realise that the sadness and grief I was going through was so overwhelming that I could not see the positives. Without consciously acknowledging it, I was slipping into a depression.

I know I should have been building on the momentum from work and the financial stability that appeared to be just around the corner, but every time I knew I should push on I found a reason not to. I always justified it to myself that it did not matter and I hid behind the sadness of my grief. Time to stay in my safe zone for a while. Obviously different timeframes come in for different people. What seems acceptable for some people will not work for others, but for sure after a year you really have to think about moving on. All the anniversaries have passed and you somehow have to contain and pigeon hole the grief so that life can go on.

I was still only six months into my grief and I was using it for all the wrong reasons. At no time did Vanessa or the kids ever say anything. They let me work through it at my own pace. They were always supportive, but I know now that I struggled and should have tried to deal with it better. I was trapped in my melancholy with no easy escape. I was functioning, but not to the standard I should have been, and definitely not to the standard my family deserved.

The stepping stone of Rental Number Eleven was coming to an end and we had not resolved anything. I was not in a position to make any life changing decisions with regard to buying a home. If anything, we had gone backwards. I had used the time to grieve but had achieved precious little else. We had burned through $24,000 on rent in six months, had a branch fall through the car window during a storm, I had neglected work, and my enthusiasm and self esteem were at an all time low. For the first time in my life I had started to question the reality of how difficult my life had become. If it was not for the love of my wife and family, things could have got very dark, and I mean permanently dark.

Because Jay Peak was not resolved, my dad's house was not selling, and real estate was slowing down, we made the predictable decision to rent again. We were good at it, why rock the boat. Just down the road on the border of Safety Harbor and Clearwater were the Sunfish Bay condos. Waterfront, pool, tennis court and a trendy three bedroom end unit, soon to be known as Sunfish Bay, loosely translated to Rental Number Twelve.

Usual spiel from the owners. They wanted to retire there in five years but we could have it for that long if we wanted. By this stage we did not believe a word of it but carried on regardless. One year lease, done.

All along in the background Jay Peak was playing out, which I always knew about because, as you know, I checked the website at least twice a day. Both defendants were in prison now, convicted in the criminal cases against them. No sympathy there.

The sale eventually went through after an auction. It sold for less than we hoped, obviously, but it would mean we would get about $100,000 back at some stage over the next few months. Everything took so long because it had to be approved by a judge, so it would be at least six months before we saw any of that.

You know how I talked about life's ebbs and flows and how they were completely out of balance with our needs? When we had money behind us, all the wheels of creating more income would grind to a halt. When we had no money, they would crank back up and create enough for us to survive. Never to prosper, only to survive, and this has been our experience the whole time we have been in the US. We take two steps forward and then two and a half steps back, followed by two steps forward and one and a half steps back. Money wise we never got anywhere, we still haven't, but somehow through it all we survived, and more importantly that is the bigger picture we need to focus on. That is our journey, to survive. Not glamorous at all, I know, but there must be a reason for this, a reason we are still looking for.

So it all sounds woozy to get $100k, but when you have not earned much in the previous six months and have relied on credit cards to get through, it does not go far. Paying off the credit cards, leasing a car, paying lease fees to move

SIXTY NOT OUT

and all the other expenses involved with keeping a family of five functioning in today's America is not cheap. That $100,000 will probably buy us twelve months of living the American Dream. You see, the thing here is it is all pretty fake. You have to fake it till you make it. Successful and well off people attract successful and well off people. If you are one of the have-nots, then most of the time people do not want to know. It is all about perception. If you look successful and behave with confidence, almost arrogance, then it is assumed you are that person and like minded people are attracted to that.

You set the expectations and it is assumed you are that person. It is only ever skin deep. It is very rare people take the time to peel away the layers and get to know the real person behind that flashy car or in that expensive house, because, as we know all too well, that is a manufactured illusion, a fake life and just part of the bigger picture that is at play here in modern America.

We know. We live it. We try to play the game, but it is an expensive game and one that not everyone is going to win. Us included.

In a nutshell, when we have money our income dries up. When we have no money and the debt is racking up, fate sees to it that we are given just enough to survive. Rinse and repeat for ten years. It all makes for an interesting life.

But what is the bigger picture? We are so used to this cycle now, feast or famine, it is almost like we have become complacent. Expecting something when we have nothing and when things are good we know it will be short lived. We have become conditioned to expect the opposite, which really makes for a screwed up mindset.

Real estate was quiet, but I eventually got a small inheritance from the sale of my dad's house. Real estate picked up again and I had hoped it would coincide with the private litigation being finalised. We were hopeful, but at the last minute, just as the case was beginning, a settlement was agreed. For a few weeks the possibility of a decent payout had been diminishing. History would suggest that any time you are up against politicians with a reputation to uphold or a state agency, then it is going to be tough. The small guys never win, right?

It was eventually negotiated that the settlement would not only apply to the named plaintiffs, of which I was, but also to everyone else caught up in the fraud, some eight hundred people. So the settlement figure was a lot smaller than I had hoped. Once the attorneys had covered their expenses, which were considerable considering the whole action had taken over two years to litigate, we were left with a pittance. This was a huge blow because I had naively believed we would get more. The attorneys did okay, of course. The defendants did better than okay because they did not have to acknowledge any wrongdoing and completely dodged a bullet. It is so evident and obvious that they did not fulfill their remit, which was to monitor, oversee and audit the whole Jay Peak investment on a regular basis. They failed miserably, were complicit and then hid behind big brother when the day of reckoning came. Shame on them and their lack of accountability and shame on the judicial system for not better protecting the little guy.

Feast, famine. On it goes. This is no way to live. There has to be a better way, but for now that is all we have.

Over our years in the US, we can probably count on one hand when our life scales have been balanced. What I mean by that is no debt, some savings, a healthy family and steady work. For our first few months at Sunfish Bay we probably checked all those boxes. The only slight niggle was the post pandemic crazy real estate market had ground to a halt and my yearly wages were starting to slip drastically. I probably did not pay as much attention to this as I should have. Comfortably numb springs to mind. I just assumed it would get better. I was guilty of short sightedness. No debt and some savings, life was good. We even booked an all family trip to Italy, that is how good it was, or so I thought.

But it really was not. We were again burning through money. I refused to acknowledge that it would all disappear. I was holding on for that one big real estate deal that was bound to come. But it did not.

SIXTY NOT OUT

I mean we are not talking about an overnight crash and burn scenario. We were blessed to be supported by a successful business Vanessa had established ten years prior, which gave us great cash flow, especially on the pre-holiday run up from late October through the end of the year. But this probably fuelled my denial even more as it bought me an extra three months to land that elusive real estate deal, which had a canny knack of remaining elusive.

We renewed the lease again after twelve months as it was the easiest thing to do and the tax return from the previous year had shrunk significantly. We probably did not qualify for a mortgage on these overpriced homes anyway. Also, they were now starting to come down in price and it did not seem like a sound investment at the time to commit money into a falling asset. That is one way I justified it anyway. Another was that we probably could not afford it and another was did we even want to be in America anymore? We had tried and tried relentlessly over many, many years to make a success of it and it was proving to be very hard work, soul destroying and a battle we possibly would not survive. Ultimately we would have to make a decision to stick or twist, but for now we would bury our heads in the sand for another year and pray that the goose would eventually lay some sort of golden egg.

I do not think our trip to Italy helped with the big question mark over our future. It was refreshingly nice to get away with the family, to spend quality time with the family and immerse ourselves in the rich culture of another country, basically to escape the day to day mundane existence that our lives had taken on in the US. I am not blaming the US entirely as I am sure fifteen years in any country could lead to boredom, repetitiveness and the bursting of the zest for life bubble. But if you add into the equation the whole Jay Peak experience then it boils down to our initial decision to come to the US.

It is our fault for choosing the US, but it is not our fault what happened to us once we arrived here. We have just found it extremely difficult to deal with the circumstances we have been dealt. We have survived, barely. We have had pockets of fun and good times, but on the whole it has been a huge struggle filled with sadness, stress and anxiety. I wish to God that we had not come here, but we did.

It was a decision we made in good faith, but it turned sour pretty quick, and it is only the strength of our family bond, the five of us, that has enabled us to still have the dream of a better future.

The equilibrium of the scales did not last too long. Not long after the Italy trip the savings were dwindling and right on cue our latest landlord joined the ranks of all the yo-yo landlords we had ever had and decided he and his wife missed their condo so much that they wanted to move back in. They were nice enough to say that if we found something quickly they would let us break the lease without any penalty, which was extremely pleasant of them as it would also enable them to move back in even quicker.

The thing is, with the owners telling us we have to leave, it gives us no opportunity to make the decision for ourselves. We are always having to be reactionary, which means our choices are limited. If it were our choice then it would be something we wanted to do, which would make it fun, well almost. When we have no choice, it is really not fun and involves a lot of resentment and anxiety. We end up having to make do with what is available at the time within our budget, and it does not always give us much of a choice.

Nicely set up for Rental Number Thirteen. Nice location, in a nice neighbourhood just over the road from the last, but it would be a struggle to call it a nice home. It is pleasant but very old fashioned, in need of a makeover to join the current decade, if not century. Anyway, welcome to San Domingo Street. Cheap and cheerful.

By now we had streamlined our lives down to the bare minimum to survive. We were a family of three essentially, surviving with just one car, a bit of a shit pit for a home, and it was mutually decided that our youngest was to be home-schooled. This was a combination of exorbitant private school fees which we had paid the previous year when the scales were balanced, and a window of about three weeks when the universe aligned to make homeschooling look like the only option. She was having a tough time with friends at school, registration for the next year was closing and her best friend was going online as well, it all made

SIXTY NOT OUT

sense. Things change, but at that exact moment in time when decisions have to be made, it was the sensible choice.

We were a lean, mean family machine. All the frippery was eliminated, it was time for a reset. I had left my original broker after ten years and after a brief blip with a friend who started a new brokerage, I ended up joining an all singing, all dancing team with a fantastic reputation and the prospect of good things to come. Maybe that goose would eventually lay that golden egg.

The Jay Peak debacle was on the back burner. All that could be resolved had been resolved and the only thing in the future would be a small final payment once the receivership was wound down. This meant that after all these years of checking the website a ridiculous number of times every day, I was now down to once every month or so. I can even say that sometimes weeks would go by without me even thinking of Jay Peak. Progress had definitely been made. It had been such a big part of our lives for fifteen years now, the majority of those bad, but what had happened had happened and there was nothing anyone could have done to change the outcome. I have beaten myself up so much over the years at the detriment of my family and my wellbeing, but it is something that is behind me now. I must learn to look to the future. After all, I am only sixty and I still have a lot of living to do.

- 24 -

Making Sense of Everything

Sixty not out. It is a reference to a batter in cricket; a stupid title really, especially considering I don't play or, quite frankly, even like cricket. But it somehow seemed apt. The sixty part is self-explanatory, but the "not out" part is very appropriate considering what our family has been through over the last fifteen years.

I think my early life and adventures were so perfect that any disappointment in later life would resonate a lot harder. You have a lot further to fall if you have already reached the peak of the mountain. I'm not just talking about money, either. I'm talking about family, wife, kids, and life. I truly did have everything, but what's the point of having everything at 45? That's way too young to just settle or be content. There was so much more life out there, more living to be done, more adventures, more excitement, and ultimately more risks to take.

Life is a journey. It is a cliché, I know, and probably used way too often as a throwaway line. But until you actually live that journey and fully understand what it means specifically for you, it takes on a whole new meaning. If you are lucky enough, it begins to make sense. It gives you a purpose that helps validate decisions you made when, in all reality, you could not justify them at the time.

Life's journey begins to make more sense the older you get...obvious statement, I know...but it's only in later life that you have the opportunity to use that journey as self-therapy.

I started writing this book about six months ago, when I was still consumed by guilt, anger, and regret about the whole Jay Peak thing. I thought it would be therapeutic to put all my disappointment down onto paper as a way of channeling the turmoil and sadness I had built up over the previous ten years. It was similar to writing a letter to someone and then burning it on top of a mountain; some sort of absolution. I somehow had to rid my soul of the negativity Jay Peak had created.

My initial thought was that the book would be solely about Jay Peak and how it had affected me and my family. As an afterthought, and to add some context, I thought it important to establish who I was as a person before our American adventure. I planned on writing a few chapters about my childhood and my life with Vanessa and the kids before moving to the US. You know, set the scene of a nice family life, and then the majority of the book would be made up of hate and anger towards Jay Peak, filled with a "woe is me" attitude, wallowing in self-pity and guilt.

The thing is, the book started to mirror my life. I thought it would be filled with what had consumed me over the last ten years...or more importantly, what I had let consume me...but as I progressed, I realised that the last ten years were only a small part of my journey. I had given them star billing and more airtime than they deserved. As I remembered all the adventures, experiences, and, dare I say, escapades I had gone through as a young man, all the heartfelt, genuine moments with my wife and kids, successes in business, the balance of the book started to change. Each little memory seemed to unlock another memory; things that were locked away in the far reaches of my mind and, if it hadn't been for me sitting down to write this book, they possibly wouldn't have surfaced, ever.

The pages I had dedicated to talking about sadness, anger, and guilt were being replaced by pages of happiness, laughter, fun, and a little mischief! The

     SIXTY NOT OUT

therapy was working. By reminiscing on my journey, I began to feel thankful for my life, what I had achieved as an individual, and what I had accomplished as a husband and father. My whole mindset changed 180 degrees (no, I'm not a landlord) throughout the writing of this book. The vitriol and hate that was planned disappeared, and I truly took pride in remembering how blessed a life I had led, and continue to live.

Don't get me wrong, I still resent what happened to us, but I'd like to think, for the most part, that I've come to terms with it. If things get a little dark, I throw around the odd quote that we say as a family, "fake it till you make it," or in our case, "fake it till you fail!" Or on a more personal level: Made in Hong Kong, perfected in Wales, and broken in the US. I'm going to ask the girls to put that one on my headstone when I'm dead and gone...although I would prefer to be cremated, but that's a topic for another time!

It's funny how, when you are faced with addressing your emotions and trying to put them into words, you have that moment of clarity. The sense of dealing with something in your mind and recording it on paper is so therapeutic. So often we think of things, dwell on them, try to make sense of them, but it's only when you take a second to write them down and think about those words that they make complete sense. Quite often recently, I've found it beneficial to zone out and do a little meditation; maybe it's two minutes while I'm working out or brushing my teeth, just to shut the world out and go into David's world. It is so relaxing. I'm convinced Vanessa thinks I'm falling asleep, just as my dad did. I don't think he could help it, but I consciously shut my eyes and take time to process what I want to do next or, as I found with this book, think about positive memories and how I can best translate them onto paper. It's super important to write them down quickly before I forget; something to do with those drugs in my early years, I wouldn't wonder!

I found I was much happier and much more inspired to write about the positives from my life than dwell on negativity. It was also a lot easier to write about happy stuff. After all, there is a lot written about Jay Peak online that I didn't want to bore you too much. If you wanted to dig deeper, you could easily serve up a fair dose of unpleasantness yourself. You can even say that you now know someone who was affected by it...and he turned out okay, just.

So here I am, sixty and still going. I've achieved something I always said I wanted to do: write a book. One off the bucket list. I always thought it would be fiction; Tommy Tenpence was way up on the list for quite a while, but real life had a way of changing that. My conversational memoir has proved to be both therapeutic and cathartic. See, it was the right word! It's taken me from feeling sorry for myself to acknowledging that life is complex and life is cruel, but foremost, life is for participating in, good or bad. So enjoy it for what it is, even on the shitty days or during the shitty weeks and months. Try to stay positive. Easier said than done, I know, but hopefully there is a sunrise on the horizon for all of us.

I'm not sure what's next for us. That will be determined by family, both here and back in the UK. But what I do know is that even if you feel like you don't have anything materially, if you have family, then you have everything. You have everything money can't buy. I knew this already, but it was probably about time I was reminded, and Jay Peak reminded me the hard way.

I'd like to think that my sixties will be full of book-worthy experiences. I know I'm not ready to stop searching for all that life has to offer, I'm excited to see where my kids end up and where Vanessa and I eventually decide to settle. Who knows, we may be in a position to buy a home sometime. Whether that will be in the US remains to be seen, but if I can fill the next ten years with fun and excitement and all the things life throws at you...or even just a fraction of what I went through over the last sixty...then another book could be on the cards. Let's just hope I will be able to remember it all. Maybe I will call it something like "Seventy, Not Out." It has a certain originality about it, I feel. I'll keep you posted!

Acknowledgments

Writing this book began as something very different from what it ultimately became. It started as a place to put my frustration, my anger, and my disbelief at how life can turn on a sixpence. What I didn't expect was that the process of writing it would reconnect me to the people and moments that truly define me. And for that transformation, I owe some very important thanks.

First, to Jodi at Shine Press. As a first-time author stepping into completely unfamiliar territory, I had no idea what I was doing. I had a story...raw, emotional, and at times chaotic...but no roadmap for how to shape it into a book. Jodi walked me through every stage of the process with patience, clarity, and steady encouragement. She answered questions I didn't even know I should be asking. She turned overwhelm into structure, doubt into momentum, and a manuscript into something I'm proud to hold in my hands.

Publishing your first book is a vulnerable experience. There are moments when you question whether your story matters, whether anyone will care, whether you've said too much or not enough. Jodi never let me lose sight of why I started. Her belief in the project, and in me, made all the difference. I am deeply grateful for her professionalism, her guidance, and her calm voice when I needed it most.

Most importantly, this book belongs to my family.

To my wife...my partner through every high and every low...you have stood beside me with strength and grace that I can barely put into words. You have shared in the excitement, absorbed the stress, and carried the weight of uncertainty without ever letting me feel alone. When everything felt like it was slipping away, you reminded me of what truly matters. Your support wasn't loud or dramatic...it was steady, constant, and unwavering. That kind of love changes a man.

To my three daughters, you are the heartbeat of this story. Every chapter of my life has meaning because of you. The adventures, the risks, the setbacks, the comebacks...none of it would hold the same weight without the joy, laughter, and perspective you bring into my world. You have given me purpose far beyond career or ambition. Watching you grow has been the greatest privilege of my life.

Without my family, this book would have no relevance and no reason to exist. It would simply be a collection of events. You are what gives those events meaning. You are the lens through which I see success and failure. You are the reason resilience matters. You are my grounding force and my motivation to keep going.

This memoir may carry my name on the cover, but its spirit belongs to all of you.

You are my everything.

www.ingramcontent.com/pod-product-compliance
Lightning Source LLC
Chambersburg PA
CBHW071510140726
47997CB00005B/1930